YOU ARE HERE FOR A REASON

This year, we come to *Matan Torah* carrying more than we expected.
This is not just an eighth edition. It is a response to the reality we are living in,
the strength we were asked to find within ourselves, and the quiet, steady voice
that says, keep going.

You are here, opening these pages, and that already matters. Something in you
chose this moment, and I want you to know
it was created with you in mind.
Here in *Eretz Yisrael,* as these pages came together, rockets were falling,
not as background noise, and not something distant, but with real intention to
harm. The times are uncertain, and in the middle of life, we are producing and
launching this beautiful, self-funded startup from the *mamad* (shelter).
It is a true labor of love, coming from all our hearts, from *neshama* to *neshama*.
It is a miracle that we are here. That we are okay. We move quickly in Israel.
We do not stay stuck. We do not remain in fear. We continue to live, build,
create, and move forward. But we cannot move forward without saying clearly:

Thank You, *H-shem*.

Thank You for protecting us, for the open miracles we witnessed,
and for giving us the strength not only to endure, but to keep building, because
this magazine is part of that.
H-shem is the true CEO of this project.
The incredible women you will encounter here were not chosen by me, they
were chosen by *Him*, at the exact moment they were meant to meet you where
you are.
It's a space of connection, growth, and reflection, where Jewish women from
different backgrounds and journeys can sit together, learn from one another,
and grow. Every woman who said yes brought her heart, her wisdom, and her
care, with the intention that something here will reach you and uplift you.

As you read, think about your own receiving.
Think about the story of *Ruth,* and where you find yourself within it, your journey,
your choices, your relationship with *H-shem*, your connection to *Torah*.
Nothing is as dear to us as *Torah*. This is what we celebrate.
As someone who chose this path, I feel that deeply. I am proud and honored to
bring you this eighth edition of Her Tribe Magazine, a bestie, a retreat in print.
A hub for hashgacha pratit. Every story here holds a world.
What you are holding is a spark, meant to awaken something within you. Read
this like a conversation, like a quiet moment that belongs just to you.
Find yourself here.

Like a flower in bloom, may something within you open in this season, gently, in
its own time, receiving, growing, and carrying forward the light of *Shavuot*.
You arrive as you are.
You show up, still becoming.

Chag Sameach.

Naomi Journo &
The Team

IYAR:

THE MONTH OF HEALING

How This Sacred Month Invites Us to Heal, Grow, and Connect Heaven to Earth

BY: DALIA ORLEV

We have crossed the threshold of Passover — we have tasted freedom, felt the winds of liberation, and now we find ourselves in a tender, in-between space. This is *Iyar*, the second month of the Hebrew calendar — known in *Kabbalah* as *Chodesh HaRefuah*, the Month of Healing. This is not coincidence. It is design. The very name *Iyar* is

an acronym for the divine promise in Exodus 15:26: *Ani H-Shem Rofecha* — "I am the Lord who heals you." G-d does not say He will heal — He says He is healing, continuously, right now. *Iyar* is the living proof.

A BRIDGE BETWEEN TWO REVELATIONS

Iyar sits precisely between two monumental spiritual events: the freedom of Passover in *Nisan* and the receiving of *Torah* at *Shavuot* in *Sivan*. In *Kabbalah*, the Hebrew letter of *Iyar* is the **Vav** (ו) — shaped like a connector, the bridge between heaven and earth. The *Vav* connects two dimensions of your inner life: what you **know** and what you **live**. It asks: Is the wisdom you carry actually flowing into your daily life?

THE TRIBE OF ISSACHAR: WISDOM THAT MUST BE LIVED

Each Hebrew month is associated with one of the twelve tribes (*Sefer Yetzira*), and *Iyar* belongs to **Issachar** — the contemplative tribe described in Chronicles as "knowers of understanding the times." *Issachar* did not simply study *Torah*; he knew what to do with it.

"FROM THE SONS OF ISSACHAR, THOSE WHO HAD UNDERSTANDING OF THE TIMES, TO KNOW WHAT ISRAEL OUGHT TO DO."

—CHRONICLES I, 12:33)

The *tikkun* (soul-correction) of *Issachar* is the gap between *Chochmah* (wisdom received) and *Da'at* (wisdom integrated). We are blessed with more *Torah* and spiritual teachings than ever before — yet how much truly lives in our daily choices? *Iyar* invites us to close that gap through *hirhur* — contemplation that turns knowledge into transformation. Ask yourself: **What wisdom am I learning but not living?**

COUNTING THE OMER: DAILY HEALING, DAY BY DAY

All of *Iyar* is held within the ritual of *Sefirat HaOmer* — Counting the *Omer*. For 49 days between *Passover* and *Shavuot*, we count each day, refining one soul-attribute at a time: lovingkindness, discipline, compassion, endurance, humility, connection, and sovereignty. In *Kabbalah*, *sefirah* shares a root with "sapphire" — a radiant, luminous stone. To count is to polish. This is *Iyar's* healing: not the dramatic healing of a crisis, but the gentle, daily polishing of who we are becoming.

YOUR HEALING OPPORTUNITIES THIS IYAR

Iyar is also called *Chodesh Ziv* — the Month of Radiance. Here are five ways to work with this sacred time through the **O.R.L.E.V.** Healing method:

OPEN TO POSSIBILITY: It Is Never Too Late. *Pesach Sheni* (14th of *Iyar*) carries an eternal message: no matter where you have been, you can always return. Healing has no expiration date. Journal your intentions for healing this month.

RELAX AND REENERGIZE: Walk in Nature. The trees are blossoming and releasing phytoncides — natural compounds that calm our nervous system and support immunity. Step outside and feel where heaven meets earth.

LEARN AND LISTEN: Study Something and Apply It. Choose one piece of wisdom — from *Torah*, a class, or a book — and ask: "How does this apply to my life right now?" Share it with someone. This is the work of *Issachar*. This is how wisdom becomes healing.

EXPERIENCE JEWISH MINDFULNESS: Settle Your Mind. *Rabbi Nachman of Breslov* taught that distance from G-d comes not from negative traits, but from an unsettled mind. This month, pause.

Breathe. Your Divine consciousness is already within you — it only needs space to surface.

VISUALIZE: Notice and Elevate Your Traits. Spend a few minutes each day in *hirhur*—contemplation. Ask: *Which shadow trait needs my attention?* With compassion, elevate it to its Divine Source, remembering that even in darkness there is a spark of light. Then visualize yourself embodying its opposite positive quality—the trait *H-shem* is guiding you to live today.

As we move through these 49 days of inner refinement — from the birth of freedom at *Passover* to the receiving of *Torah* at *Shavuot* — may we use the bridge of *Iyar* wisely. May the letter *Vav* do its holy work: connecting what we know to how we live, connecting our human striving to Divine guidance, connecting heaven to earth — right here, right now, in our very own lives.

Dalia Orlev has been teaching Jewish Wellness programs for 45 years. She is the founder of the O.R.L.E.V. Healing Method and creator of many Jewish Meditation and Movement programs. A certified Jewish Meditation Teacher and Holistic Therapist based in Efrat, Israel, she teaches Jewish mindfulness live and online to Jewish women worldwide.

daliaorlev@gmail.com
Jewish-mindfulness.com

Sivan:
The Quiet Power of Integration

BY: YAEL DWORKIN

BY SIMCHA EVEN CHAIM I THE LIGHT OF THE MOUNTAIN I SIMCHA-ART.CO.IL

There is something subtle about the month of *Sivan.*

It does not arrive with the drama of *Nissan*, with miracles and release. It does not carry the slow inner work of *Iyar*, with counting and refinement. *Sivan* arrives quietly. And yet, it holds one of the greatest moments in history: the giving of the *Torah*. But perhaps its true power is not only in the moment itself, but in what makes that moment possible.

Kabbalah teaches that *Sivan* is the third month, and that this thirdness is not just numerical. It is essential.

There are always two forces in life: expansion and contraction, giving and holding back, light and shadow. We live inside these tensions.

So often, especially as women, we feel pulled between them: wanting to give and needing to protect, wanting connection and needing space, wanting to be seen and fearing exposure.

The instinct is to choose one side. To become either all-giving or fully guarded. Either strong or soft. Either independent or relational.

BUT *SIVAN* WHISPERS SOMETHING DEEPER.

You are not meant to choose. You are meant to integrate. In the language of Kabbalah, this is called the middle path, the ability to hold opposites without collapsing into either one.

It is the space where kindness does not erase boundaries, strength does not block love, and vulnerability does not weaken identity. It is not compromise. It is wholeness.

Sometimes walking the middle path feels like integrating fire and water, two forces that cannot meet directly. Left alone, they extinguish each other. But place a vessel between them, and something new is created. Warmth. Nourishment. Life.

> **There are always two forces in life: expansion and contraction, giving and holding back, light and shadow. We live inside these tensions.**

THE VESSEL IS THE MIDDLE PATH.

And this is the deeper meaning of *Sivan*: the creation of an inner vessel that can hold complexity without breaking. When the people of Israel stood at Mount Sinai, they are described in the singular, as one person with one heart. This was not only unity between people. It was an inner unity. A moment when fragmentation quieted. A moment when the internal voices, the doubts, fears, and contradictions aligned enough to receive something higher. Because truth cannot enter a divided vessel.

THERE IS SOMETHING DEEPLY FEMININE ABOUT THIS WORK.

A woman lives this tension constantly. She holds life inside her while still being herself. She gives deeply while sensing her own limits. She navigates emotion, intuition, thought, and relationship, often all at once.

She knows, sometimes without language, that life is not linear. And yet, many women have been taught, subtly or directly, to split themselves. To give without receiving. To soften without boundaries. To hold others without being held. *Sivan* comes to correct that.

Your power lies not in choosing one side of yourself. Your power lies in becoming a space where opposites can meet safely.

The inner quality of this month is movement. Not standing. Not escaping. Movement.

Movement implies direction, intention, and growth. It is the shift from instinct to awareness. From reacting to choosing. From being pulled apart by inner contradictions to gently holding them and moving forward anyway.

This is not dramatic change. It is quiet, steady steps, the kind no one sees but that shape a life.

At the heart of *Torah* is a paradox. We are created with a deep desire to receive, and yet we are called to become givers.

So what do we do with that tension? The answer is the middle path.

To receive in order to give. To allow ourselves to be filled with love, with support, with truth, not as an end, but as a flow.

For many women, this is the deepest work. To receive without guilt. To take in without shrinking. To allow nourishment without immediately turning it into output. Because only a full vessel can truly give.

EACH YEAR, *SIVAN* RETURNS.

Not just as a date on the calendar, but as an invitation.

To stand again at your own inner Sinai. To gather the scattered parts of yourself. To soften the inner conflicts. To become, even for a moment, one person with one heart.

And in that quiet alignment, to receive.

Yael Dworkin, recently of Montreal, has been a Judaic studies educator for nearly three decades. Her love of *Torah* and *chassidut* inspires her to share its depth with others seeking growth in their *Avodat H-Shem*. Since her *aliyah* to Israel in 2019 she has taught at *Shiviti, Midreshet Rachel v'Chaya, Neveh Yerushalayim*, OU Israel Center and was the Educational and Program Director of *Shevach Torah* and Art Program.

Yaeldworkin@yahoo.ca

yss-shevach.learnworlds.com

THE FIRES, THE FLAGS, AND THE FAITH

LIVING YOM HAATZMAUT, LAG B'OMER & YOM YERUSHALAYIM IN ISRAEL

BY: RUTI EASTMAN

During normal times, I might attend a *brit milah* in the morning, welcoming a new little boy into the world, then a *vort* celebrating my neighbor's daughter having found her true love, followed by a *shiva* visit to comfort a friend who lost her father, ending the day with a wedding or a *bar* or *bat mitzvah* celebration. How life-affirming! Being permitted a seat on the rollercoaster of Jewish life, being embroidered into the tapestry of other people's lives! That is exactly why *Yom HaZikaron* coming the day before *Yom HaAztma'ut* is so challenging, but also deeply meaningful. "There is no other place in the world where a nation cries together one night, and dances together the next."

I love watching Israeli flags go up all over my small *Gush Etzion* town. Blue and white flags hanging on car windows, fluttering on banners, on apartment buildings and houses. There are charcoal and *mangalim*—small, disposable barbecue grills—in nearly every shopping cart leaving the grocery store. The singing and streetside bands, the smell of barbecuing beef and chicken, make the entire town feel like we're all at one big party. And, of course, we are: Everyone around us is celebrating the gratitude and fierce pride we feel, in ourselves and in our family members, for the faith and fight it takes to hold this precious Land.

I feel this more, year after year, as my sons have grown from being rowdy teens to frontline soldiers with small children of their own. There is perhaps no time that I see us as *"Ish echad v'lev echad"*—one person with one heart—as much as I do on Israel's Independence Day.

At the midpoint of the spiritually introspective *Omer* count comes a day that my sons always loved. It is *Lag B'Omer*—the 33rd day of counting the *Omer*—a holiday that commemorates the end of a plague among *Rabbi Akiva's* students and honors the passing of *Rabbi Shimon bar Yochai*, a renowned sage and mystic. But to my sons and most of the other kids I know in Israel, it is the night all of Israel goes up in flames, in the most positive sense.

SIMCHA EVEN CHAIM I RABBI SHIMON BAR YOCHAI I SIMCHA-ART.CO.IL

Bonfires are a way of symbolizing the spiritual light and wisdom that *Rabbi Shimon bar Yochai* brought into the world through his teachings, particularly the *Zohar*. Many people, over the 18 years we have been privileged to live in Israel, have traveled to the holy city of Meron to immerse in the spiritual tension and joy of remembering these holy men. Some of my sons attended over the years and were awestruck by the sheer numbers of attendees. But most years, they stayed close to home, enjoying local *Lag B'Omer* celebrations.

In the America of the 1970s, there was a public service announcement (popularized by a Jewish radio announcer, incidentally) that reminded parents to be aware of what their kids were up to during the late-night hours. "It's ten o'clock. Do you know where your children are?"

On this unique night, we know exactly where our children are. They are huddled near bonfires wherein every unguarded piece of wood "stolen" by kids over several preceding days is set ablaze under the watchful eyes of roving parental guards. The parents are there to be sure their little pyromaniacs don't singe off their eyebrows and to discourage them from tossing aerosol cans into the fire "just to see what will happen." These kids may not spend a lot of time thinking of the great rabbis of ages past. But they will sing joyful songs and celebrate simply being alive in the holy Land of their forebears.

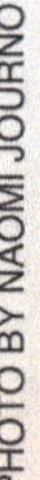

Yom Yerushalayim follows, only a week before *Shavuot*. If *Yom HaAtzma'ut* celebrates the Land of Israel and *Lag B'Omer* celebrates our national Soul, *Yom Yerushalayim* celebrates our collective Heart. It is held to honor the day after the Six Day War when we reclaimed the Jewish people's holiest city. There is a mystical magic to walking through this City in the evening, when the sun begins to depart and brushes the Jerusalem stone with a soft pinkish-orange farewell kiss. In normal times, there will be *Rikud-Dgalim*—the "Dance of Flags"—parades through the streets of the City, along with musical and religious celebrations. In normal times, the *Kotel* plaza fills with celebrants, thanking G-d for once again allowing us access to this very holy place, this fragment of our past that still connects us with our Holy Temple.

During these difficult days, the fires and gatherings may be more subdued. Our sons and daughters may still be fighting. As of this writing, I await a precious message each day from my son's unit that says they're still okay. I can breathe again… for a few more hours,

until the next message comes…and the cycle begins again. His brave wife takes care of their children, rushing them to the safe room when the sirens blare. Family members keep each other's spirits up.

The Jewish people will continue to celebrate our existence together. We will celebrate the many miracles G-d has bestowed upon us, some obvious and some less apparent, but very clearly stamped with His hand. May we continue to show Him that we have learned the lesson *"B'yachad nenatzeach"*—only together will we be victorious—and may we see the complete redemption of the Jewish people in this holy Land and throughout G-d's world, speedily and in our days.

Ruti Eastman: After serving in the US military, Ruti Eastman married her hero, discovered Judaism, and homeschooled four sons. The family made *aliyah* to Neve Daniel in 2007. She is a published author and poet and teaches harmonica and percussion. Ruti has recently been published in the acclaimed *Az Nashir* series.

rutimizrachi@gmail.com

Wake Me When October's Finally Over is available on Amazon. In Israel? Contact me directly for a copy.

My Aliyah Story:
A Leap of Emunah

BY: SAM KRAMER

The Moment Everything Aligned

Our *aliyah* story was not one big decision. It was a series of moments that slowly built on each other until it felt undeniable, like *hashgacha pratit* guiding every step.

When we first started thinking about it in May 2021 and **started** working on getting our older kids on board, everything depended on one very practical piece: my husband's job. I knew I would not be able to continue working as a public-school teacher in the same way, so if he could not work remotely, this would not happen.

We started preparing quietly. We made plans, sold our house, and went on a pilot trip. At the same time, something deeper was happening under the surface.

It was the period following COVID, alongside the rise of the Black Lives Matter movement, and there was a noticeable shift in the atmosphere in the U.S. We saw increasing antisemitism in ways that felt close to home, like Jews being attacked while sitting at outdoor restaurants. At the same time, while travel to Israel wasn't possible, we felt a stronger pull than ever to be there.

With our oldest getting closer to high school, it started to feel like now or never.

Then came the moment that changed everything.

It was *Ta'anit Esther*. I was sitting and *davening* while my husband went in to speak to his boss. I remember feeling like *Esther*, walking into something uncertain but knowing it was completely in *H-shem's* hands.

About thirty minutes later, he called me. "I don't know what just happened."

He had gone in with a careful plan. A one-year trial, remote work, maybe some travel. Something safe.

Instead, his company told him they had, unbeknownst to him, already been thinking about opening an office overseas and wanted him to lead it.

In that moment, everything shifted. It felt unmistakable. Like *H-shem* was saying, you are making *aliyah*.

Looking back, it was not one reason. It was everything coming together at once practical, emotional, and something deeper that is harder to explain but very real.

Building a Life From Scratch

We made *aliyah* in 2022 from West Hempstead, New York, with five kids and no real plan beyond knowing that we were supposed to be here.

We came completely alone, but my closest friends who had made *aliyah* before us stepped in as our family here.

As hard as that was, it is also what made it so meaningful.

When you come with five children, you do not have the luxury of easing in slowly. Every decision matters right away. Schools, friends, language, routine. Everything.

It was intense. But that intensity forced us to build a real life here very quickly.

At the same time, our family showed up in the ways that mattered. My parents came to help us land and later made *aliyah* themselves, and we've stayed closely connected to the rest of our family.

For me, one of the hardest parts was losing my professional identity. I had spent sixteen years building something very clear. I knew what I was doing, and who I was through that work. And then suddenly, none of that translated.

No one here knew what I had done or who I was. That feeling was uncomfortable, but it was also honest. It forced me to ask new questions. What do I actually want to build now? Who am I in this place?

I started to see how many women go through this. That process of rebuilding, not just practically, but internally.

What helped me most was *emunah*, and people. Slowly, things started opening up in ways I did not plan. My path today looks different. Less structured, more self-driven. But it feels more like mine.

There was one moment early on that really stayed with me. A friend I had just met invited me on a women's trip to *Maarat HaMachpelah*. It was a random Monday morning.

I remember thinking, this is normal here. This is what life in Israel feels like. You do not have to create meaning. It is already built in. *Torah*, *tefillah*, history; it is just part of your regular day.

Being part of an established community helped more than I expected. There was already a rhythm we could step into. Things like the *Tekes Maavar* between *Yom HaZikaron* and *Yom Ha'atzmaut*, which we did not fully understand at first, became deeply meaningful over time.

If I could go back, I would put more effort into building relationships earlier. Community does not just happen. You have to choose it.

Living With Meaning

There were also things that unfolded that I never could have planned.

After October 7, everything shifted. In some ways, it slowed our integration. But in other ways, it deepened it completely.

I created Israel Good News Only as a WhatsApp group because I needed it. I needed a place to focus on something positive in the middle of everything that was happening.

What started as something small grew into a global community. At the same time, I started traveling more, especially to the south. Visiting soldiers, meeting families, just being present.

That experience changed how I see this country. When you meet people in the *Otef*, on *kibbutzim* and *moshavim*, who went through everything and still chose to come back, you understand something deeper. Their connection to the land is not abstract. It is lived.

That stayed with me. It also led me somewhere new. I completed the Ministry of Tourism tour guide certification course and started traveling the country more intentionally, learning its stories, its history, and its depth.

What started as living here turned into wanting to really understand it, and eventually share that with others.

Life here feels different in ways that are hard to explain unless you live it. Conversations are deeper. People speak about *emunah*, about the future, about purpose, in a very open way.

There is also a different value system. Less focus on status, more on connection. Less about what things look like, more about what they are.

Here, we do not have to explain who we are. My children are growing up in a place where being Jewish is the default. Where it is public. Where it is part of everything.

We are raising them in the middle of something real. One thing that keeps me grounded is choosing to look for the good. Not in a naive way, but in an intentional one. It is very easy to get overwhelmed here. Focusing on the good keeps me connected to why we are here.

That mindset became something I acted on, not just something I thought about. Watching our kids become part of Israeli life has been one of the most meaningful parts of this journey. Joining *Ezra* gave them a natural entrance to a social group. Even when English was spoken, Hebrew was always there, through the *madrichim* and *madrichot*, through everyday life.

Things like *Lag BaOmer*, community events, *davening* for soldiers; these are not special occasions. They are just life.

If I can say one thing to anyone thinking about *aliyah*, it is this: You do not need to have everything figured out. But you do need to be willing to let go of control.

Build your network early. Ask for help, even when it feels uncomfortable. Choose a place where your family can land softly. (Feel free to reach out to me for guidance or *chizuk* on your *aliyah* journey.)

Things will not always work the way you expect. You might go to three stores to find one thing. It is not Amazon.

But what you gain is something else entirely. Life here is more personal. More connected. More real. If you feel that pull, it is there for a reason. Come.

Sam Kramer is the founder of **Israel Good News Only**, a global media platform that began as a neighborhood WhatsApp group created to share uplifting news during challenging times. Now reaching over 34,000 members worldwide, it connects audiences through WhatsApp, Instagram, and a newsletter. Visit her website to find the links to join.

- **sam@sam-kramer.com**
- **@israelgood_newsonly**
- **www.sam-kramer.com**

Ra'anana: The Geography of Belonging

BY: SARAH LEAH (SUSAN) EKLOVE

A Moment That Reveals a City

It's Friday night, the first *Shabbat* since the beginning of the war with Iran. My husband wants to go to *shul*, but there are restrictions, as people need to stay close to their shelters. He finds out there is a minyan happening at the corner of the street and leaves the house. Moments later, I hear the singing of *Shabbat* prayers entering my home through the open windows. So many voices. It's so beautiful.

I walk to the end of the street and am in awe as I see hundreds of men, women, and children lining the street, welcoming the *Shabbat* Queen. I stand under the moonlit sky and palm trees, surrounded by neighbors, only some of whom I know, who have stepped out of their homes, a stone's throw from their safe rooms. I breathe in the smell of orange blossoms and take in the moment, the feeling of togetherness and unity in the midst of this war. To me, this is a typical, magical moment that captures Ra'anana, a small city where people truly come together.

The Journey

I grew up in Toronto, Canada, and had been dreaming of making *aliyah* since I first came to Israel at the age of 18 in 1983. It took over thirty years, but in August 2019, just after our 30th wedding anniversary, my husband and I made *aliyah*.

We had three grown daughters living in Tel Aviv and Jerusalem, and one of them had recently spent a *Shabbat* in Ra'anana and felt it might be a good fit for us. We came to check it out and immediately connected to the feel of the community. It's a small yet well-established city (Hebrew: רעננה, lit. "fresh") in the southern *Sharon* Plain of Israel's Central District, offering a high quality of life, and it has everything one might need. There was something familiar about it, a blend of the suburban lifestyle we knew in Toronto with the warmth and landscape of Miami, yet unmistakably Israeli, with Hebrew on every storefront. With our grandchildren just a half-hour away, traffic permitting, we thought, let's try it, and we stayed.

A City of Many Voices

Ra'anana is a living example of *Kibbutz Galuyot*, the in-gathering of exiles. On its streets, you hear Hebrew alongside English in many accents, as well as French, Spanish, Portuguese, and more.

The city is very *aliyah*-friendly, with an excellent *ulpan* that offers not only language learning but also a sense of belonging. My classmates came from all over the world. There are also part-time learning options, making it accessible for different lifestyles.

Ra'anana is diverse in every sense, with a wide spectrum of religious expression. There are many *shuls*, often reflecting the communities that founded them; American, South African, Syrian, and others, each contributing to the rich communal fabric.

Community in Action

One of the most striking things we noticed as we got to know the community was the culture of *chesed* and volunteerism. People show up for one another. There are countless WhatsApp groups, requests for help, offers of support, and shared events and information flowing constantly.

There are also many opportunities for learning and growth. A special gem for women is *Matan HaSharon*. The year after Corona, I gave myself a "seminary year" and attended daily. It was an incredible experience, learning, connecting with women from across the city, and improving my Hebrew. *Matan* offers both English and Hebrew classes, along with programs, events, and even a monthly musical *Hallel*.

Life and Practicalities

Although we moved after raising our children, Ra'anana offers a wide range of schools. One standout institution that bears mentioning is *Beit Issie Shapiro*, a center for children with special needs that draws families from across Israel. It offers therapies, innovative services, and even a dental clinic. *Beit Levenstein*, a major rehabilitation hospital, is also located here.

At the western edge of the city lies Park Ra'anana, a beautifully maintained and expansive green space that offers something for everyone. With its tranquil lake and small boating area, a charming animal corner, wide open lawns, and thoughtfully designed playgrounds, the park creates a perfect balance between nature and community life.

Whether you come for a quiet stroll, a family outing, or a moment to unwind, it captures the relaxed and welcoming spirit of Ra'anana.

Finding Your Place

Ra'anana is shaped like a long rectangle, approximately five kilometers in length, with its main street, *Ahuza*, lined with shops, cafés, and restaurants. There is also a mall and a country club, and because the city is relatively flat, it is highly walkable, except in the summer heat.

People tend to settle in smaller pockets, often centered around specific *shuls* or schools. While the city is mixed, secular and religious, with *Olim* from around the world, there are general patterns. The northeastern area tends to have more Americans and Canadians, while the north-central to western parts have more South African and British communities, along with a *Kollel*. Still, every area is a blend, with Israelis and *Olim* from many backgrounds living side by side.

Many people choose Ra'anana because they are seeking community. Since there are multiple sub-communities, finding the right fit takes research. Thankfully people are incredibly open and eager to help newcomers connect to neighborhoods, schools, and resources.

Housing

Compared to smaller towns or *yishuvim*, Ra'anana is considered expensive. There are various

housing options, from older apartments to newer developments and private homes, but prices are on the higher side.

At the same time, Ra'anana offers a unique balance. It feels like a small town, yet everything is within reach. It is large enough to offer variety, yet small enough to feel manageable and comfortable.

There are many *Olim Chadashim* in Ra'anana, which means many people are looking for friendship and community. That openness is beautiful, but building relationships takes effort. It really is starting over again, and it takes time.

I bless you that wherever you choose to build your life in Israel, your *aliyah* should be smooth and peaceful, and your journey filled with meaning, connection, and joy.

Sarah Leah (Susan) Eklove is a sound meditation facilitator, teacher, writer, life coach, and Jewish meditation guide. Drawn to the healing power of sound, she integrates vibrational instruments with Jewish wisdom. She leads workshops from her home in Ra'anana and works part-time at *Havat Marpeh*, supporting October 7 trauma survivors.

shmoozinwithsusan@gmail.com

@Soulsoundswithsusan

Susie Stearn Eklove

Friends, Falafel, and Starting Over in Israel

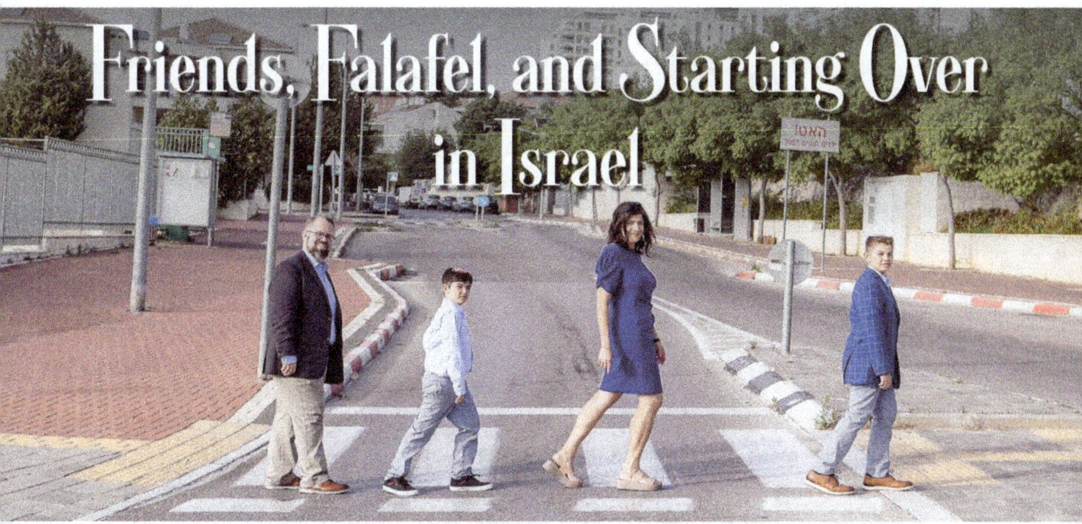

BY: SHARON WEISS-GREENBERG

No one really tells you this before *Aliyah*, but the biggest shift isn't just language, bureaucracy, or even schools.

It's not a full reset. Sometimes, in unexpected places, you run into someone from your past. A former student, a camper, a colleague you barely knew. Suddenly, you are both here. That familiar face matters more than you would have imagined. It is comforting. It is grounding. And sometimes, it becomes something deeper the second time around.

Here is what actually helps.

1. LET GO OF "HOW IT WAS," EXCEPT MAYBE AMAZON

You will miss things from back home. For me, losing decent online shopping was rough. Israel is not built for seamless, two-day delivery. Even after COVID, it is still not quite a thing.

But it becomes a game. One day, you walk into a completely unrelated store, and there it is. The exact item. Every store sells what it sells and then other completely random items. Lean into it. The "haha" moment replaces the convenience.

2. DO NOT WAIT TO FEEL SETTLED TO BUILD A LIFE

If you wait until your Hebrew is strong, your paperwork is done, and your home is set up, you will wait too long.

Life here happens while things are unfinished.

Volunteer. Say yes and show up even when you feel like you do not fully belong yet.

3. IF YOU DO NOT WANT TO BE LONELY, BE INTENTIONAL

I do not like being lonely. So, I decided not to be passive about it.

I build one-on-ones. Small groups. Bigger gatherings. You can make great friends in the most ordinary places or by joining a community *bet knesset* or sports league. I invite first and figure it out later.

I have become known as a connector. It brings me joy and meaning, and it turns out, people here appreciate it. Israelis are busy, but they are also very into living life to the fullest. If someone creates an opportunity to gather, people respond.

Whatever your version of that is, go for it.

4. YOUR PAST LIFE SHOWS UP IN HELPFUL WAYS

I did not realize until I moved here how ready I was for this. The skills you have built over time do not disappear. They translate. You may feel like a beginner, but you are not starting from nothing.

5. OLIM ARE A NETWORK. USE IT

There is an immediate understanding among *olim*. Even if your backgrounds are different, you share a common experience. These are often the people who will answer your questions, share tips, and remind you that you are not alone.

Build those relationships. They matter.

6. ASK FOR LIFE HACKS AND ACCEPT THEM

People here share information freely. How to deal with customer service, where to go, what to say, and when to show up.

One of the best tips I learned: skip calling customer service and go straight to WhatsApp. Always double-check hours before you go anywhere. Better yet, call or email too. Offices may be open two to four hours a week, or only at very specific times. Do not assume anything.

Israel is another world in some respects, beyond the language. Learn it, and your life becomes easier.

7. LEARN THE SOCIAL RHYTHM

Israel is direct, fast, and informal.

People may cut lines. They may speak bluntly. I do not like line-cutting. I probably never will. But I have learned to stand my ground.

You may sound like an immigrant. Speak anyway. If you stand with confidence and know your basic rights, people respect that.

Confidence carries more than perfect Hebrew.

8. BUILD BEFORE YOU BELONG

Connection here does not always happen organically. You create it. Follow up after meeting someone. Suggest coffee. Invite people even if it feels early. Some of my closest friendships started with slightly bold invitations.

9. YOU MAY ALSO BE LEARNING HOW TO LIVE THROUGH A WAR

This is part of life here. What would be considered a major crisis elsewhere is, in Israel, woven into daily life in a way that can feel disorienting.

You may experience whiplash.

There are stretches that feel like lockdown. You are more alert, more aware of where you are and where you need to go. And then everything reopens. Schools resume. People go back to work. You meet for coffee. Life picks up within hours.

And still, there is community. People check in. Neighbors show up. WhatsApp groups become lifelines. There is a shared understanding that you are part of something bigger, even when it is hard.

You learn how life continues alongside uncertainty.

10. YOU MAY NEVER FULLY "FIT IN," AND THAT IS PART OF IT

Even years in, you may not catch cultural references. It takes effort in a way it never did before being an immigrant.

You might go back to visit where you came from and feel slightly out of sync there too.

On the upside, you become a lifelong learner.

11. NOTICE THE GOOD, BECAUSE THERE IS A LOT OF IT

People help each other. Kids look out for one another. Strangers are never strangers; they step in. These moments are not small. They can make everything else worth it.

Aliyah is not smooth. It is layered, surprising, sometimes exhausting, and often meaningful in ways you did not expect.

You may not fully "get it." That is okay. Somewhere along the way, you stop feeling like you are visiting. You participate. Then build. Then you belong.

And one day, you realize you are no longer waiting. You are living here.

Sharon Weiss-Greenberg is an executive leader, educator, and nonprofit strategist. She serves as Vice President of Development at The Next Step, chairs the board of *Magen*, and is a sought-after fundraising consultant. She has held leadership roles across major Jewish organizations and is committed to children's rights, education, and philanthropy.

sharonweiss@gmail.com
sharonweissgreenberg.com

EXCLUSIVELY FOR HER TRIBE MAGAZINE

Sunny Levi's path is built on discipline, but not only the physical kind. An eighth-degree black belt in Taekwondo, her journey evolved into something deeper: a life rooted in Torah and a conscious relationship with *H-shem*. As a mother of six and an *Emunah* coach for women, she teaches how to align body, mind, and neshama through practical, consistent steps.

Having her wisdom in print is a gift. We are truly lucky to share her perspective here.

1. What is this season of the year inviting us into?

This is a time of renewal. A renewal of our relationship with *H-shem*, with ourselves, and with our lives. We are preparing to receive. And to receive, we need to become a vessel.

The body is that vessel. When we take care of it physically, mentally, and spiritually, we create space to receive more.

2. When women come to you feeling out of balance, what is the first step you guide them to take?

The first step is always to slow down and come back to the present moment. We do that through breath. When we focus on breathing, we begin to regulate the mind and our thoughts.

So first, breathe. Come back into your body, get grounded, and become aware.

From there, we invite *H-shem* in. Even though He is already there, we need to become conscious of it. We reestablish that connection and remind ourselves that we are not alone, and that there is a bigger picture.

When the breath slows down, the nervous system calms. That is what allows us to step out of reaction mode and return to awareness.

3. What does it actually look like to build this awareness in real life?

It takes practice. There is no quick fix. The real work is learning to pause. Usually, something happens and we immediately react. **The goal is to catch that small space before reacting and choose how we want to respond.**

Instead of judging ourselves, we can reflect. What just happened? What could I have done differently? Even that creates a new pathway in the brain. Over time, through repetition, you retrain yourself.

One simple tool is placing one hand on your heart and one on your stomach, and breathing deeply into your belly. Feel the expansion as you inhale and the release as you exhale. Try to feel your heartbeat. This brings you out of your head and into your body. It gives you a moment to pause.

4. What does a grounded, aligned day look like for you?

The way you begin your day matters. The mind is very receptive in the morning.

Many people go straight to their phone, but that can immediately trigger stress or comparison.

I start differently. After washing my hands, I sit and say *Modeh Ani*, and then I repeat it in my own words. **Thank You for giving me my soul back today.** You believe in me.

That shifts everything. You begin with connection and confidence, understanding that today is a gift and that you can handle what comes.

After that, I journal briefly, then go for a walk and do *hitbodedut*. This sets the tone for the day and puts me in a state of gratitude and connection.

From there, I hydrate, take care of my kids, exercise, and begin my work. Throughout the day, I stay aware of my needs, spiritually and physically.

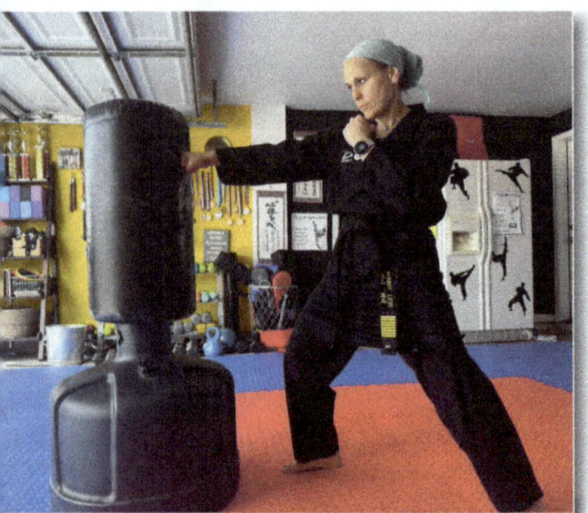

5. What allowed you to build real consistency, even in full seasons of motherhood?

A lot of it comes from years of martial arts training. I learned that even when you are not in the mood, you still show up.

But more than that, I have experienced the difference. I am a better mentor, a better educator, and a better person when I take care of myself. So it is not selfish to put yourself first. It would actually be irresponsible not to. Everyone benefits when you are regulated. At the same time, my routine changed in different stages of life. When my children were younger, things looked very different. Sometimes my time with *H-shem* happened later in the day. **Consistency does not mean rigidity.** It means commitment within your reality. And sometimes, it requires practical support. There were times I asked my husband to watch the kids, or relied on an older child, or even arranged a babysitter, just so I could step out for 15 or 20 minutes to walk and speak to *H-shem*.

I understood the value of that time, and I saw the difference in myself when I did not have it. That is what made it non-negotiable.

6. How can someone begin hitbodedut in a simple and accessible way?

A simple structure makes it accessible:

1. **Set intention.** Tell *H-shem* why you are there and ask for help to connect.
2. **Express gratitude.** Thank Him for whatever you have.
3. **Reflect.** Be honest about what is happening inside you.
4. **Request.** Ask for what you need.

Even a few minutes done consistently can be powerful. We have to remember that everything comes from *H-shem*. Not from people, not from circumstances. When we internalize that, turning to Him becomes natural. Sometimes consistency requires support. Even 15 minutes of quiet, protected time can make a real difference.

7. How do you approach resistance when something feels blocked or heavy?

First, be honest with yourself. Know your stage and what is actually realistic.

Sometimes we want something, but it does not match our current capacity or our nervous system. Ask yourself if it is sustainable right now.

When there is resistance, it is not random. It usually means something deeper is going on. It is not laziness. It can be fear, overwhelm, or not feeling safe or worthy. **Instead of forcing yourself, bring it to *H-shem*.** Speak it out. When you open that conversation honestly, you begin to understand what is blocking you. When you understand the root, you can begin to shift it, instead of fighting yourself again and again.

8. What did martial arts teach you about inner strength?

It showed me that if I can build strength physically, I can build it internally as well. **Real strength is not about aggression. It is about self-control and discipline.**

Training taught me that growth takes repetition. You fall, you get back up, and you keep going. That same process applies to inner work. Strength is built through consistency.

9. How can eating become a more conscious, connected experience?

Eating is a holy opportunity. We can eat mindlessly, or we can recognize that *H-shem* is sustaining us. When we eat with awareness, gratitude, and *kavana*, it becomes a moment of connection. Instead of forcing discipline from the outside, we work from the inside. When we align internally, our actions begin to follow naturally.

10. What are the practices that keep you anchored, no matter how full life gets?

The relationship with *H-shem*. Everything stems from it. When that relationship becomes real, it brings clarity, peace, and strength into every part of life.

- A short walk
- Drinking water
- A few minutes of connection with *H-shem* + Reading a few lines of an *Emunah* book
- One intentional meal
- Stretching with deep breathing

These small steps build consistency. Over time, they create real change. They remind you that you must show up for yourself, even in the middle of everything.

Sunny Levi is a certified emunah coach, inspirational speaker, 8th-degree black belt in Taekwondo, founder of the Spiritual Growth Bootcamp. A mother of six, she leads transformative retreats and guides women to align body, mind, and *neshama*, deepen their connection with *H-shem*, and break through limiting beliefs with practical, grounded tools.
🌐 **Sunnylevi.com**

The Edible Wellness Garden of Shavuot

BY: YSANNE SPEVACK

A Festival Rooted in the Land

Chag HaShavuot means the Festival of Weeks, and it's usually shortened to *Shavuot* — meaning "weeks." But there are older names for this spring festival, including *Chag HaKatzir*, which means the Festival of the Harvest. At its heart, *Shavuot* is an ancient wheat festival, marking the time when green wheat crops were cut and then left in the fields over the long, hot summer to ripen and dry. There's a second part, which is *Sukkot*, when the ripe grain is gathered and taken inside after drying in the fields, and ground into flour for winter.

The Rhythm Between Pesach and Shavuot

Shavuot is also a twin to *Pesach*, as the first day of *Pesach* and the first day of *Shavuot* each mark the beginning of a grain harvest. *Pesach* is the start of the barley harvest, and *Shavuot* begins the wheat harvest, which is why some Jews eat their last piece of *matzah* on *Shavuot*. It's a mirror of *Shabbat*, too, as a wheat-based pause for learning *Torah*. It falls in the seventh week of the *Omer*, just like *Shabbat* is the seventh day of every week.

The symmetry and mathematics of the Jewish edible calendar are beautiful and profound — something I see firsthand here in Jerusalem, and even more so in the fields near Haifa, where the Aaronsohn Research Farm is located and where my own culinary research has taken me.

Bringing Ancient Wisdom Into the Modern Kitchen

But how can you use this ancient agricultural geometry in your own edible garden at home — in a window box, or in your kitchen? How can we incorporate Jewish seasonal inheritance into daily life without extra expense or unrealistic time commitments? Part of my work has been trying to translate the ancient Jewish wellness diet into a modern format, so it's usable.

Wheatgrass: The Simplest Place to Begin

Firstly, we need to talk about wheatgrass, because it's perhaps the simplest and most basic ingredient of your Jewish wellness garden. Inexpensive and low on space, it's best grown on your kitchen counter, away from direct sunlight — meaning it's even possible to grow when a kitchen has very little counter space or few windows. If you have a place on the floor to leave a small baking tray, you're ready to supercharge your health with daily shots of green juice. A natural multivitamin, wheatgrass shots are full of antioxidants and help the blood absorb oxygen deep into tissues, so you'll notice cuts healing more quickly and your cheeks becoming pinker. It's anti-inflammatory, so aches and pains are soothed — and all of this can lift your mood.

A Season for Renewal and Detox

Who doesn't need a mood and immunity boost during this difficult time? *Shavuot* is the ideal time of year to detox, and it's no coincidence that the crop we celebrate is suited for this very purpose. Wheatgrass is entirely gluten-free while the grass is still young, because there are no grains in the immature shoots. I've written the recipe on page 108, from grain to green juice, with detailed instructions on growing and juicing wheatgrass at home.

Healing Herbs Already Around You

Of course, *Shavuot* also marks the start of allergy season for many — but there are so many herbs you can grow that help lower histamines in your blood, easing these symptoms. Some of them even grow as weeds in your garden, offering benefits at no cost.

Nettles are the number one remedy for hay fever and grow wild in gardens and public spaces in many climates. You're often pulling them out as weeds — but you can use them to heal your body. Take care when harvesting them, as they sting the skin. Don't risk it — wear gloves and allow them to dry in the sun. Once fully dried, strip the leaves from the stem and store them in a glass jar with a lid. Steep in boiling water and drink the infusion daily to help prevent allergies before they even begin. The *Rambam* didn't have the scientific tools we have today, yet he still understood that nettles should be a central herb in any apothecary.

Nettles don't just soothe symptoms — they can stop itching eyes and help clear the lungs due to their antihistamine properties.

Plantain is another antihistamine that grows widely, with its tall stalk rising above a rosette of leaves and topped with tiny white flowers. It can be used immediately to treat histamine flare-ups. Simply pick a fresh leaf and either chew it or mash it using a pestle and mortar. Apply the pulp directly to affected areas — whether swollen eyes or irritated skin. It works quickly, often calming the reaction within fifteen minutes.

Wellness Without Cost

The three humble weeds in this article can help keep your blood oxygenated, your body calm, and your mood balanced — without a single shekel leaving your wallet. The *Rambam* prescribed it all freely, with simplicity and wisdom. Enjoy this time-honored Jewish approach to wellness for *Shavuot*.

Chag HaKatzir Sameach!

Ysanne Spevack is the author of a dozen cookbooks, with reviews in *The New York Times, Jewish Chronicle,* and *Daily Mail.* She's writing a book about ancient Jewish food, including the wheat harvest that's central to *Shavuot,* and the deep symbolism that's integral to wheat, from Jacob's Ladder to *challah.*

Before the Table Is Set:
Creating a Home Ready for *Shavuot*

BY: SHOSHANNA STEIN BENARROCH & REBEKAH SALTZMAN

BECOMING THE HOME
The Inner Work of Preparing for *Shavuot*

BY: SHOSHANNA STEIN BENARROCH

As we get closer to receiving the *Torah* on *Shavuot*, it's not only about receiving its wisdom or keeping the *mitzvot*. It's about something deeper. It's about becoming someone more elevated and creating a space that can actually hold that elevation. We're not just cleaning, managing, or creating ambiance. We are creating an environment where *H-shem* can dwell.

"**ושכנתי בתוכם**" *Veshachanti B'socham, Shemot* 25:8, "And I will dwell among them", not in it; in us. The home becomes an extension of who we are, physically, emotionally, and spiritually.

Meaning, whatever is happening inside of you will naturally be reflected in your space. Your inner world and your outer world are constantly mirroring each other.

You can feel the difference immediately.

When everything is scattered, your mind is scattered.

When the space is calm and in order, something settles inside of you.

You can think, you can breathe, and you can be present.

The *Torah* teaches us that beauty is not extra.

"**זה קלי ואנוהו**" *Zeh Keili V'anveihu, Shemot* 15:2, "This is my G-d and I will beautify Him."

Honoring *H-shem* includes making things beautiful. A space prepared with care, attention, and intention softens us. It opens us and draws us in.

There's also a difference between clean and peaceful. A peaceful home creates *menuchat hanefesh*, an inner state of calm, settledness, and emotional ease. Our body relaxes, our energy shifts, and we end up showing up differently.

The *Torah* is **אור**, light, but light needs a place to land. When a space is chaotic, it doesn't settle. When it's clear, intentional, and cared for, that light rests there

naturally. So on *Shavuot*, we're not just receiving the *Torah* again. We're asking, where is it going to live? Cleaning becomes making space. Organizing becomes creating flow. Beauty becomes *kavod*. We're not just creating a home as a vessel for something bigger. We are the home.

Shoshanna Stein Benarroch is a teacher, artist, and mentor whose *chizuk* radiates from a deep awareness of *H-shem*'s love. Founder of the Ki Tov Project, she inspires others to seek divine goodness in every moment and see *H-shem* everywhere. Find her

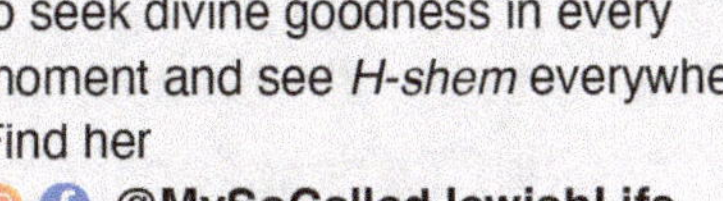

@MySoCalledJewishLife. The Kitov Journal

Creating Flow at Home

PRACTICAL SYSTEMS FOR A CALM AND ORGANIZED SHAVUOT

BY: REBEKAH SALTZMAN

Preparing the home for *Shavuot* is not about doing everything. It is about creating clarity and flow so the home can actually function with ease. When you know what needs to be done and when, the entire atmosphere shifts. You move from pressure into calm, and that changes how you experience *Yom Tov*.

START WITH A CLEAR MASTER CHECKLIST.
Write down everything, meals, shopping, cooking, hosting, and final setup. This becomes your roadmap. Once it's on paper, you stop relying on memory and start working with structure. That alone reduces stress and keeps you focused. It also gives you a visual sense of what can be done now, what can wait, and what can be handed off to someone else.

PLAN YOUR MEALS INTENTIONALLY.
Choose a manageable menu and build your shopping list directly from it. You do not need endless variety. A clear plan saves time, avoids overbuying, and makes cooking feel controlled instead of overwhelming. My approach is especially practical here: even if you like to cook more

freely, a written list still helps the person shopping know exactly what is needed. That removes confusion and saves follow-up questions in the middle of a busy day.

BREAK PREPARATION INTO CATEGORIES. Do not mix everything together. Finish your shopping plan, then move to food prep, then to setting up your space. When you group tasks, you stay efficient and avoid that scattered feeling of jumping from one thing to another. Checklists also help you pivot when life throws something off. You may not be able to control every part of the day, but you can stay grounded because you already know the larger map.

USE LISTS TO DELEGATE. When tasks are written clearly, you can hand them off without needing to explain every step. This allows your family to participate in a real way and takes the pressure off you to carry everything alone. A written list also makes it easier for others to help well, because they know what success looks like.

CREATE A SIMPLE FLOW FOR THE DAY BEFORE YOM TOV. Decide what needs to happen early, what can wait, and what must be done last. Think in terms of sequence. If you know the order of the day, you waste less energy deciding in the moment.

TAKE A FOCUSED APPROACH TO DECLUTTERING. You do not need to do the entire house. Clear the spaces that impact your daily function most, especially the kitchen, counters, dining area, and any surface that tends to collect clutter. When those areas are in order, the whole home feels more manageable.

USE WHAT YOU ALREADY HAVE BEFORE BRINGING IN MORE. Once things are sorted, you often realize you do not need extra containers, tools, or supplies. Repurposing what is already in the home keeps preparation simpler and prevents adding more to manage.

FINALLY, THINK IN TERMS OF SYSTEMS YOU CAN REUSE. The same preparations come back each year. Keep your lists, refine them, and build a rhythm that works for your home. An organized home for *Shavuot* is not about perfection. It is about clarity, structure, and creating a space that allows everything, from preparation to hosting, to flow naturally.

Rebekah Saltzman is a personal organizer, coach, and author of Organized Jewish Life. She helps women create calm, clutter-free homes through smart systems and a sustainable, *Torah*-aligned mindset. Through programs like Tidy Together and Painless *Pesach*, she guides women from chaos to clarity. She lives in Israel with her family.

 balaganbegone.com

 info@balaganbegone.com

 Organized Jewish Life

From Expectation to Presence

LEARNING TO TRULY RECEIVE IN RELATIONSHIPS

BY: CHANA DEUTSCH

FOR MARRIED WOMEN

Receiving Your Spouse, Not Your Expectations

What does it mean to truly receive your spouse, instead of relating to him through expectations or assumptions?

So many of us carry a secret picture in our minds of who our spouse is supposed to be. It forms over time, from the home we grew up in, from what we wished had been different, and from things we absorbed throughout our lives through conversations, books, and observations. Slowly, almost without noticing, we build an idea of what marriage should look like and who our partner should be.

And then there is the person in front of us.

Not an idea. Not a role. Not a character.

A real person, with his own story, his own way of seeing the world, his own thoughts and emotions. Someone who will never fully match the picture we once held.

That gap can feel uncomfortable.

We may catch ourselves comparing, noticing what is missing, measuring what is happening against what we thought would happen. In those moments, it becomes harder to really see the person in front of us.

Receiving your spouse invites something different.

It is a gentle shift. A willingness to look again, not through the lens of expectation, but through the lens of reality. It means allowing space for his humanity, his strengths,his differences, and even his imperfections.

It does not mean ignoring what is difficult or lowering your standards. It means choosing to meet what is real. And sometimes, that includes his vulnerability, which can be threatening and not always easy to face.

Over time, many relationships slip into autopilot. We assume we already know the other person. We think we know what he will say, how he will respond, what he is feeling. Slowly, the relationship can begin to feel predictable, even distant.

But the truth is, both of you are always changing.

Choosing your marriage again is not dramatic. It is about staying curious, gently leaning in, and asking, even after years together, who is this person in front of me today?

What is he thinking? What is he feeling? What has shifted for him?

And also, who am I today?

That curiosity brings life back into the relationship. It opens space for deeper emotional, physical, and spiritual connection. Not because everything is perfect, but because there is presence.

Another concept that confuses many of us is the idea of acceptance.

Passivity feels like giving up. It carries the sense that nothing can change.

Acceptance is something else entirely.

Acceptance involves seeing what is actually happening, clearly and honestly. It does not mean you like it. It does not mean you agree with it. And it does not mean you have to stay exactly where you are.

It means you are no longer fighting reality.

And from that place, something opens.

Instead of reacting automatically, you can pause and ask yourself, what do I need here? What is being asked of me? What support would help?

That is where real growth begins.

Trying to control or change your spouse often creates the opposite effect. It brings tension and closes things down. But when there is acceptance, there is space. And within that space, something softer and more real can grow.

So how do we bring more connection into the day-to-day?

Often, it is in the smallest moments.

A quiet check in with yourself. How am I feeling right now? What do I need?

And then a gentle check in with your spouse. How was your day? What is on your mind?

Sharing, even in simple ways. Not waiting to be asked, but allowing yourself to be known.

It does not have to be big.

A warm hello.

A soft smile.
A moment of real attention.
These small gestures carry something deeper.

They create warmth.
That warmth builds connection.
And over time, that connection becomes steady, real, and growing.

At the heart of it, a meaningful marriage is not about finding someone who perfectly fits what you once imagined. It is about learning to truly see, and truly receive, the person who is already in front of you.

FOR SINGLE WOMEN

Becoming Someone Who Can Receive Love

What does it mean to prepare not just for marriage, but to become someone who can truly receive a relationship?

It is easy to think that preparation means finding the right person. But in many ways, it begins somewhere much closer.

It begins with you.

With learning how to check in with yourself in an honest and gentle way.

What am I feeling?
What do I want?

When you are connected to your inner world, something shifts. You become more grounded, more open, more present. From that place, connection becomes much more natural.

This is not only about a future marriage. It shapes how you experience dating right now.

You begin to trust your choices more. To whom it feels right to say yes... To whom it does not. How to show up in a way that feels aligned.

These are not just dating skills. They are relationship skills.

Because when you can listen to yourself, you can also listen more deeply to someone else. You bring curiosity, presence, and awareness into the interaction.

Many un-married women carry a picture of what marriage is supposed to look like. And that is natural.

But it can help to soften that picture.

Instead of focusing on details, begin to ask different questions.

- What do I want my marriage to feel like?
- What kind of home do I want to create?
- What kind of life do I want to build?

When you focus on the experience, something opens.

You begin to align yourself with your internal vision. And it becomes easier to recognize when something feels right.

Because someone can seem to match everything on paper and still not feel aligned. And someone unexpected can feel deeply right in ways you did not anticipate.

As you become clearer within yourself, you begin to notice more.

Not just what someone says, but how they show up. What matters to them. How you feel in their presence.

Do you feel at ease? Do you feel open? Do you feel like yourself?

Or do you feel like you need to adjust or force something to fit?

The more you trust that clarity, the more natural your choices become.

And slowly, preparation becomes less about searching outside of you, and more about becoming someone who can receive something real when it arrives.

Because in the end, relationship is not about perfection. It is about presence and alignment.

Chana Deutsch is a relationship expert and coach. She specializes in helping women foster the connection, intimacy, and love they desire in their marriage and in their home. She teaches practical, grounded strategies that support women in connecting to their authentic and vulnerable selves.

- **absolutelyfeminine@gmail.com**
- **chanadeutsch.com**

Motherhood with Clarity and Calm

BY: ORPAZ LEVY

Motherhood can often feel like a constant state of reacting. To the needs, the noise, the pressure, and everything happening around us. But real calm and confidence don't come from controlling everything outside of us. They come from how we build our home, how we lead, and how we show up within it. When parents are a united front, working together to lead a stable and loving environment, children receive the safety and security they need and a child's nervous system can settle into calm instead of staying in constant stress mode.

When *emunah* and *bitachon* in *H-shem* are the narrative of daily life, children internalize that they are safe and that everything will be okay. "Everything is from *H-shem* and everything is for the best" becomes not just something we say, but something we live.

Systems, Routines and Tools for Moms

That sense of safety is strengthened through structure. Consistency and predictability allow the brain to feel calm and regulated. When we know what to expect, stress is reduced. Routines and systems create this for both us and our children, while minimizing mental overload and decision fatigue.

- Give kids a kiss goodbye and a *bracha* before leaving the house, even a message for teens works.

- Have a consistent bedtime routine with dimmed lights, a calm atmosphere, saying the *Shema*, and including love, hugs, kisses, and bonding time. Sharing experiences from the day promotes positive emotional brain wiring.

- Set simple, predictable systems for meals, laundry, and daily flow so everyone knows what to expect.

- Use music and dancing to elevate the mood and connect with your children.

- Designate "low-power mode" days with simple meals and reduced expectations.

- Wake up to a clean, organized space to create morning calm, because our brains thrive on order.

- Schedule dedicated time for yourself, your marriage, your children, and family connection.

- At the *Shabbat* table, share gratitude and thank *H-shem* for *chesed* and miracles from the week.

- One of the most powerful tools for chaotic moments is the 20-second hug. In the middle of chaos, when kids are dysregulated, you stop and hug for at least 20 seconds. This regulates both your nervous system and your child's, while strengthening connection. It is a simple, free tool that creates immediate impact.

Mom Tribe

Structure supports the home, but support sustains the Mom. Finding time for anything in our busy lives feels impossible, but when something becomes a priority, we find the time. Creating a "Mom tribe" has to be intentional, because it is an essential need of motherhood.

Rabbanit Yemima Mizrachi teaches that an important woman is driven by what is truly important, while one who lacks clarity is constantly reacting to what feels urgent. This distinction shifts how we live and parent.

Connection with other women is not a luxury. It is a real emotional need. It allows us to share, gain perspective, and remember that we are not alone. When we prioritize this, we recharge ourselves and show up better. Our children learn that relationships and meaningful connection matter.

Tip for Turning Tantrum Time into Bonding Time

During a tantrum, a child's brain is not in a state to listen or reason. The emotional brain is in charge. Instead of letting the child lead the moment, we must lead with intention.

An emotional transition creates a quick shift in attention. You might start an engaging story, point something out, or use playful physical interaction. The goal is not to dismiss the emotion, but to interrupt the emotional loop. Once the brain settles, the child can regulate. And when they are calm, that is when they need connection the most. A hug, a kiss, and closeness restore their sense of safety. A child's nervous system mirrors ours. When we stay calm, we help them regulate. This is what it means to lead, guiding them out of chaos into connection.

Trust Your Instinct More and Worry Less

Moms don't lack instinct. They often lack confidence in it. The belief that motherhood should come naturally can lead to unnecessary self-doubt.

H-shem gave us *binah* and natural instincts, but they are meant to be developed.

Trusting your instinct means strengthening it through knowledge, experience, and clarity. It is okay not to know. It is okay to learn and seek guidance.

As understanding grows, instincts become more reliable. They are no longer reactive, but grounded. When intuition is combined with learning, a Mom moves from doubt into clarity and confidence.

Becoming a Kli – Preparing to Receive

Before *Matan Torah*, *Am Yisrael* prepared themselves to become a *kli*, a vessel capable of receiving *H-shem's* light. It required readiness and intention.

Motherhood is the same. We prepare ourselves to become a *kli*, open and connected, asking for *koach, chochma, bina, da'at, shefa, brachot,* and *chesed* to guide our path in *chinuch.*

When a vessel is empty, it has nothing to give. Filling our *kli* is essential. From that place, even daily life becomes elevated. We give from fullness, passing on *Torah* and *mitzvot midor l'dor,* from generation to generation.

Like water, *Torah* flows through every part of life, filling us, guiding us, and naturally flowing into our homes.

Orpaz Levy is a *baalat teshuva*, originally from Chicago, who made *Aliyah* 11 years ago and is a mother of eight living in Efrat. She is a parenting educator specializing in early brain development and a certified neuroscience coach, empowering moms with practical, science-backed tools and wisdom, and leading meaningful *challah*-baking experiences.

 @orpazlevy
 orpazlevy@gmail.com

When the Roles Begin to SHIFT

A PRACTICAL GUIDE TO CARING FOR AGING PARENTS

BY: LISA MARCUS

IN MEMORY OF MY FATHER DAVID ISMAN Z"L, ON HIS 13TH YAHRZEIT

Caregiving does not begin with a decision. It doesn't start with a clear moment when you say, "Now I am taking this on." It happens slowly. A parent repeats something. A medication runs out. You notice the fridge is empty. At first, you don't think much of it. You tell yourself it's nothing. But then it happens again. And again. At some point, you realize this is no longer occasional. It is a pattern.

That was my experience. I didn't have a roadmap. I stepped into it by reacting. Something happened, I dealt with it. Then something else happened. Before long, I was constantly putting out fires. And that is one of the biggest mistakes. We stay in reaction mode.

In *Torah, kibbud av va'em* is often translated as honoring parents, but the root *kaved* means heavy. It is meant to feel like a responsibility. The question is how to carry that weight without it taking over everything.

FROM CONSTANT REACTION
TO STEADY STRUCTURE

At a certain point I realized that reacting is not a system. It creates urgency, pressure, and the feeling that you are always slightly behind.

What helped was introducing simple structure. Not complicated, just consistent. Making sure there is always food in the house. Checking medications before they run out. Keeping track of appointments ahead of time. These are small things, but they change the entire experience. When there is structure, there are fewer emergencies, and more calm.

There is also denial. We aren't always ready to admit that our parents are aging. We say, "It's just a moment." But ignoring it only delays what we will have to deal with anyway.

THE EMOTIONAL WEIGHT
AND REALISTIC EXPECTATIONS

Emotionally, this is not simple. There is often a subtle, constant feeling that you are not doing enough. No matter how much you do, there is always something more.

But caregiving cannot be built on guilt. It has to be built on what is sustainable. There is a concept of *maspik tov*. Good is enough. Not perfect, not everything; but enough. We need to ask ourselves honestly what it is costing us. Because if it costs your health, your relationships, and your stability, it is not going to hold.

We also have to recognize that we cannot do this alone. We often think we should, but that is not realistic. Knowing how to ask for help is part of the process.

WHAT MAKES EVERYTHING
EASIER LATER

The conversations we avoid are often the ones that make the biggest difference later. Medical decisions, financial access, legal authority. These are not easy topics, but they are necessary.

When these things are clear in advance, everything becomes calmer. You know what your parent want. You know where things are. You don't have to make decisions in confusion or under pressure. And it is not only about documents. It is also about understanding them. What matters to them. What they would want if things change.

DISTANCE, SIBLINGS,
AND REALITY

When parents live in another country, the situation becomes more complex. You cannot just go over when something happens. You rely on systems and on people. You need a network. Someone who can check in. Someone who can go to appointments. Sometimes that means paying for help, and that requires a mindset shift. We are not able to be everywhere at once.

Caregiving also brings family dynamics to the surface. Siblings think differently, communicate differently, and have different capacities. Trying to make everything equal usually creates tension.

What works better is clarity. Each person takes responsibility for what they can do well. One handles finances, another medical, another communication. There is enough to do for everyone.

Communication style also matters. Some people need everything written down. Others prefer a conversation. Awareness of that makes things smoother.

WORKING WITH
YOUR PARENTS,
NOT AGAINST THEM

One of the biggest shifts is accepting that you cannot change your parents. Even when you are right, they may not listen. They still see you as their child.

Before *Pesach*, my mother refused to allow her caregiver to eat rice. It became a real issue. I explained, my husband explained, nothing helped.

What worked was understanding what mattered to her. She respected *Rabbanim* and doctors. So we brought someone she respected, who explained it in a way she accepted. That resolved the situation.

This is what I call creative solutions. It is not always about explaining more It is about finding the right approach, with sensitivity and respect.

PRACTICAL REALITIES
AND BOUNDARIES

There are also very practical things that matter more than we think, such as making the home safe, removing hazards, installing support where needed. These are things that prevent serious problems.

When it comes to doctors, preparation is key. Write down questions. Go with them to appointments if possible. Ask for summaries. We all have selective hearing. For them, it is even harder.

At the same time, you need boundaries. You do not have to answer every call immediately. You can ask if something is urgent and return the call when you are able. Being constantly available is not the same as being present. Sometimes what they need most is simply to be heard, calmly and without rush.

TAKING CARE OF
THE CAREGIVER

If you don't take care of yourself, you will not be able to take care of anyone else. Caregiving can slowly take over everything,

your time, your energy, your focus. You have to continue your own life, health, relationships, routines. Not as something extra, but as something essential.

Caring for aging parents is not simple. It requires patience, flexibility, and emotional strength. But it is also an opportunity—an opportunity to show up with dignity. To bring calm where there could be chaos. To create connections in a time of change.

You do not have to do it perfectly. You just have to do it thoughtfully, with awareness, and with care. And when you approach it that way, it becomes not only something you carry, but something you can feel good about.

Lisa Marcus is a Gerontology Consultant who studied at Machon Beer Emunah in Jerusalem. For 14 years, she has led the English Speaking Seniors Program in Maaleh Adumim and runs workshops for adult children with the municipality. Originally from Sydney, she now lives in Maaleh Adumim, where her parents z"l made *aliyah*.

lisamarcus2829@gmail.com

CHOOSING TO BE CHOSEN: IT STARTED AT A *SHABBAT* TABLE

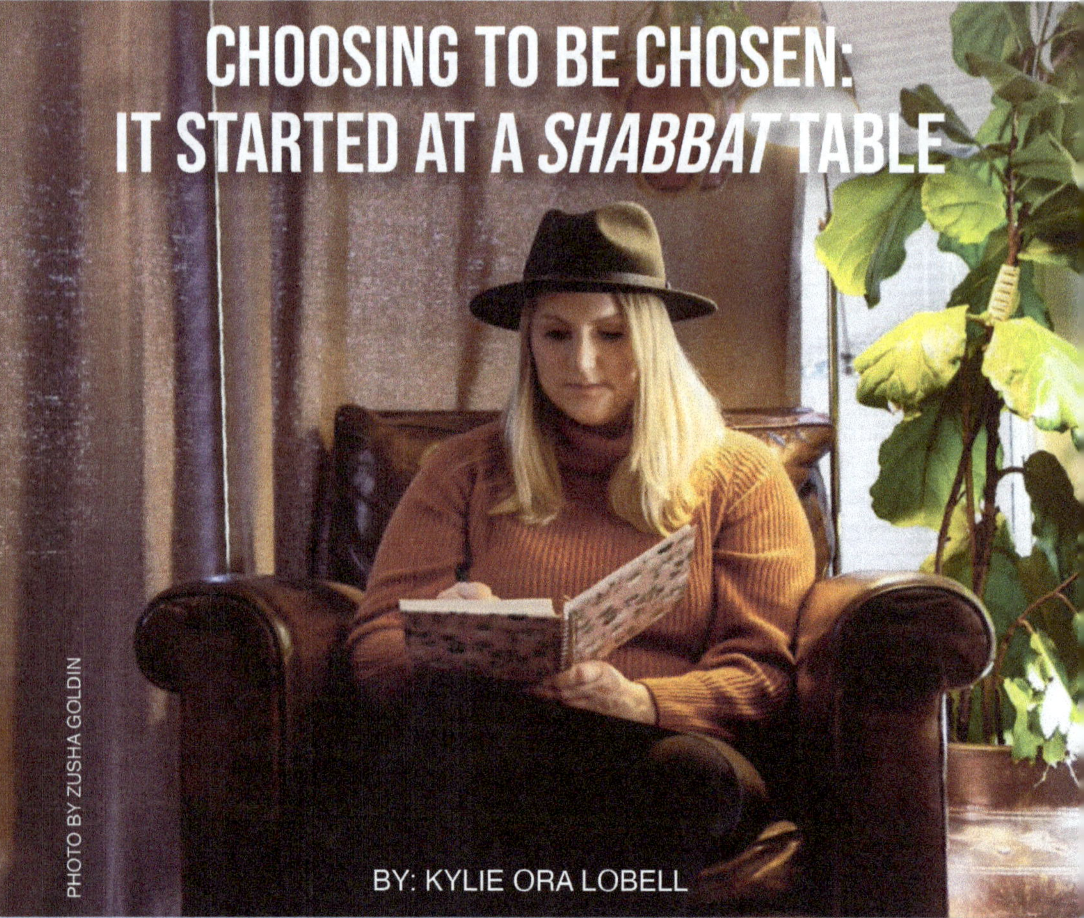

didn't grow up Jewish. I grew up in a secular Christian home in America. Religion wasn't a real part of our lives. We went to church on Christmas and Easter, but it was more about tradition than belief. As a child, I still believed in *G-d*. I prayed.

But when I was five, that changed. My parents got divorced, even though I prayed they wouldn't. When I was twelve, my grandmother got sick. I prayed for her to get better. She didn't. After that, I stopped believing.

I remember thinking very clearly, I used to believe in Santa Claus too. I learned that wasn't real. Maybe this isn't either. So I became an atheist. That decision didn't make my life better. It made everything heavier. There was no one to turn to. No one to give things over to. Everything felt like it was on me.

I was depressed through my teenage years and into college. Even when things looked good from the outside, I wasn't okay. I was getting good grades. I had internships. I was moving forward. But I didn't feel like I had a reason for any of it.

In college, I met Danny. He was Jewish but not practicing. In fact, he had walked away from it. He had difficult experiences growing up in the religious system, and by the time I met him, he didn't want anything to do with religion. He didn't even want to date Jewish women because he didn't want to be pulled back into that world.

The one thing he still kept was Friday night dinner.

One week, he said, "There's a place called *Chabad*. They have a free *Shabbat* meal. Do you want to go?" We were both broke, so I said yes. I didn't know what *Shabbat* really was. I didn't know what *Chabad* was. I didn't have any expectations. But I remember that night very clearly.

There were families, people talking, laughing, everyone engaged with each other. It was loud in a way that felt warm. It wasn't like how I grew up, where dinner was quiet. And then, in the middle of it, I felt something. I felt a warmth in my chest that spread through my body. I didn't analyze it. I didn't try to explain it. I just thought, this is *G-d*. I was twenty-one years old, and I knew I believed again. After that, I wanted to go back. Every week. That's when things started to shift.

I began learning. I had a lot of questions, and for the first time, I was in a place where I could ask them and actually get answers. Things that had always bothered me, like why bad things happen, started to make more sense.

I also started to see things differently. I felt like I could finally let go a little. Before, everything felt like it depended on me. Now, I started to feel like there was a bigger plan, even if I didn't understand it.

At some point, I said to Danny, "I think I want to convert." He didn't take that well. He told me not to go Orthodox. He didn't want to be pulled back into that life. For him, this wasn't just a new direction. It was something he had worked hard to leave behind. There was a real possibility that this would end our relationship. But I couldn't ignore it. This wasn't about him. It wasn't even about a decision I was trying to make. It felt like something I had already found.

The process took time. It wasn't one moment and everything changed. It was years of learning, adjusting, and building a new way of living.

One of the biggest changes for me was *Shabbat* because I used to be a typical workaholic, working all the time. I didn't know how to stop. Taking a full day off every week felt impossible at first. But it became one of the most important parts of my life. It forced me to slow down.

First it was just the two of us. Now we live in a strong Jewish community because we chose it intentionally. We wanted to build a life where we were not alone in what we were doing.

A friend of blessed memory once gave me the name *Ora*, which means light. I chose Ronit, a joyful song. My husband encouraged me to choose names that reflect the opposite of what I had struggled with. That idea stayed with me.

This was never only about changing what I believe. It was about transforming who I am. Today I live with a quiet certainty. I know there is something guiding my life, and I know I am not alone. I am deeply grateful to connect to *H-shem* and recognize His presence in this world. That is what I want for others as well.

I want people to feel less alone.

Writing my book and knowing that people read it, recognize themselves in it, and walk away feeling stronger, lighter, and more understood is the most fulfilling part of this journey for me. More than anything, I want every reader to take something real with them. To feel connected. To feel seen. And to feel proud, proud to be part of something bigger, proud to be Jewish.

Kylie Ora Lobell is an award-winning journalist, speaker, and podcast host of *Choosing to Be Chosen*. Her work appears in major publications including The Washington Post and Newsweek. She is the founder of KOL Digital Marketing, where she provides strategic marketing, PR, and high-level storytelling services. She lives in Los Angeles with her family.

🌐 **KOLDigitalMarketing**
▶️ **Kylie@KOLDigitalMarketing.com**
✈️ **"Choosing To Be Chosen"**
is available on Amazon

GUIDED BY LIGHT:
My Journey of Trust, Beauty, and Becoming Jewish

BY LILIANE AURA RITCHIE

There are things I have known for as long as I can remember, even before I had the words to explain them. From my earliest childhood, I felt that I was not alone. There was a presence, gentle and constant, surrounding me with a sense of safety, grace, and kindness. I did not question it. It was simply there, like light.

I grew up in the hill country of the French part of Switzerland, in a home filled with love. My father was a deeply spiritual man, and both of my parents carried a sincere connection to G-d in their own way. It was not something rigid. It was not about rules. It was something that lived in the heart. As a child, I would look at the world with wonder. Every blossom, every landscape, every waterway, sky, sunrise, and sunset felt like it was revealing something deeper. There was a sacred beauty in everything. I felt safe within it, protected, as if the world itself was filled with kindness.

As a young woman, I followed a path that looked very proper from the outside. I moved to Zurich and worked as a secretary, using French, English, and German. Everything around me was structured, precise, and disciplined. It was a very Swiss way of life. Everything was done correctly. Everything had order. There was a sense of duty and responsibility. But inside, something felt quiet and still. There was very little space for creativity, for expression, or for the kind of inner life I had always known. I could not yet fully name it, but I felt that something in me was not being lived. Still, I continued. I trusted life. I trusted that things would unfold.

Then one day, something unexpected happened. I was fired from my job without warning. It happened quickly. What I remember most is not the shock. It is what came after.

I went to sit by the lake. The sun was glittering on the water, reflecting light in a way that felt almost alive. I sat quietly and began to pray, as I had always done. And then, very clearly, I understood something. What am I doing here? What am I doing sitting behind a desk all day, when the world is so full of beauty and possibilities? I was twenty-two years old.

At that moment, I did not feel loss. I felt clarity.

Within minutes, I made a decision. I returned to my hometown of Geneva. I did not have a clear plan. I only knew that I needed to move, to explore, and to open myself to something more alive. Looking back, I see that moment as a gift. What seemed like an ending was, in truth, guidance from *H-shem*.

In Geneva, I stayed in a youth hostel. It was simple and filled with travelers. At that time, I did something quite unusual. I put up a small notice with my picture, asking if any girls would like to travel together. It was not something typical for a Swiss girl to do, but I felt free.

A few days later, a young man named Joshua saw that notice. He was traveling through Europe from California. He was Jewish, and something about him was very real, very grounded, even if I did not yet understand what that meant. That man has been my beloved husband and life partner for the past fifty years, *baruch H-shem*.

ART COURTESY OF LILIANE AURA RITCHIE I "ACCESSING BLISSFUL LOVE

At the beginning, I knew nothing about *Torah* or Judaism. Truly nothing. But through him, I began to learn. Our conversations were gentle. There was no pressure, no force. Only openness. He shared, and I listened. At times, what I learned was difficult. Hearing about what the Jewish people had gone through, and how they had been treated throughout history, was very painful. I had never been aware of it before. It was a shocking education.

But alongside that, there was something else. There was beauty.

I have always been drawn to what is beautiful, what is true, and what feels connected to *H-shem*. Slowly, step by step, I began to recognize that in Judaism. I decided to move to California to be with Joshua and get to know him better, and there I met more Jewish people and experienced more of Jewish life. It was something very natural and, at the same time, very deep. It was not something imposed. It was something lived.

Still, I did not immediately think of becoming Jewish. It was simply a process of growing closer, of understanding more, and of allowing something to unfold.

There came a moment when everything became clear. I had the privilege to meet and be connected to Rabbi Shlomo Carlebach, whose presence and guidance showed me what Judaism truly is. Through that connection, I saw kindness, warmth, depth, and a genuine relationship with *H-shem*. It was not theoretical. It was alive. At that moment, becoming Jewish was no longer a question. It felt natural. It felt right. It was not a dramatic decision. It was quiet knowing.

My conversion was not something public or celebrated in a big way. It was very quiet, very personal. I have always been a shy person, and I did not seek attention. For me, the transformation was something internal, something about the heart. It was not about being seen, i about becoming. Everyone around me was kind and supportive.

Over time, Judaism became completely natural to me. I no longer felt connected to my previous background in the same way, not because it was wrong, but because now I had grown into something that felt fully aligned with my soul. We built a family and were blessed with five children. Raising them in a Jewish home was not something I questioned. By then, it was simply who I was. It was how we lived, guided by *Torah* in a way that felt alive and meaningful.

We eventually moved to Israel, where my husband worked as a physician and professor. Life there was simple in many ways, but very rich spiritually. Being in a place where people are connected to something deeper, where life is guided by meaning, was very important for us. It strengthened our connection to *H-shem* and allowed us to grow in ways that felt natural and true.

At that time living in Yerushalayim we had the privilege to be close to the *Amshinover Rebbe*. That connection was truly life changing and enhanced the holiness of our marriage by leaps and bounds.

Throughout my life, one thing has remained constant. I speak to *H-shem*, and I listen. This is what has guided me from the beginning, not through force and not through fear, but through trust.

If there is one thing I would share, it is this: trust that *H-shem* is there to guide you. Speak to Him with your whole heart. Thank Him for the beauty in your life. Even something as simple as a flower can remind you of His kindness.

When you look at the world with that awareness, you begin to feel that you are supported, that there is purpose, and that there is love in the way things unfold.

As I began painting and writing soulful books, images, words, and ideas would emerge and flow forth, bringing me a glowing sense of purpose. There was immense joy in being able to communicate transcendent messages through imagery, colors, symbols, and story. Now I understand why I felt impelled to play with my paint brushes and colors.

Our souls have infinite depths waiting to be unfolded and explored. My heartfelt prayer is that you may enjoy receiving the profound meaning conveyed through these images and words.

Now I understand that this is part of my purpose, and what was missing at the beginning of my journey now feels complete. It is to bring joy, to share a sense of wonder, and to open a small window into those higher realities I felt even as a child..

May you discover realities worth exploring. May they bring you trust, confidence, and a sense of loving purpose. May they open doors to joy and to your immense potential, to something that was always there.

Like light.

Liliane Aura Ritchie is a multimedia artist, author, and co-founder of the Refuah Coaching Institute. A mother of five, she has inspired thousands through her books, paintings, and teachings. Her work shares messages of faith, healing, and inner clarity, guiding others to experience trust, purpose, and connection to higher spiritual awareness.

Visit my website for soulful meditation audios and inspiration.

🌐 lilianeritchie.com

🔷 Books: "Masters and Miracles," "Answers from Above: Connecting with Divine Guidance" and "A Gift of Love," can be purchased at Amazon.

FINDING MY WAY BACK TO TORAH

FROM RESISTING TO RECEIVING, FROM SPARK TO FLAME

BY: MASKIT MATI

A Question That Once Shook Me

"Where are you from? For real?" That question terrified me.

Hi, I'm Maskit, and this is my story. I had a sweet and beautiful childhood. Life was simple until it wasn't.

I was born in Israel and grew up very traditional. Not fully religious, but it wasn't all or nothing. My mom came from a religious family, my dad didn't, and we lived somewhere in between. Some relatives kept *Shabbat*, some didn't. But Friday night, you showed up. There was *Kiddush*. There was a strong sense of *Sephardic* tradition that was just there.

I sometimes joke and call it "tank tops and *Torah*." That really was my life. At six years old, everything changed. We moved to Australia. I didn't speak English. I had no friends. I found myself in a very religious school, surrounded by rules I didn't understand. After my free-spirited childhood, my world turned upside down. I wasn't rejecting Judaism. I just couldn't connect to something I didn't understand.

After a few years, we left that world completely and became very secular. I moved to a non-Jewish school, and for the next thirteen years, that was my life. From the outside, it looked like freedom. Inside, I felt empty.

I tried to fill that space with creativity. I started creating videos, dreaming about Hollywood. Filming, editing, singing, performing. I was even into cheerleading. I loved the energy, the stage, the feeling of being seen. But I also wanted to belong.

I remember that when my grandfather passed away, my mom asked me to go to *shul*. At first I really didn't want to go but when I walked in, I felt something I couldn't ignore. It felt like my *neshama* lit up. I always had a relationship with *H-shem*. I would talk to Him, even when I wasn't keeping anything. That connection never left me.

It's the same feeling I get when I'm singing, when everything in me is present and aligned. I didn't have words for it yet, but something inside me had opened.

By the time I was sixteen, I was going out, drinking, staying out late, trying to fit into a world that didn't reflect who I was. I also had non-Jewish relationships. And even then, I remember saying, almost without understanding it, "We can't really be together because I'm Jewish." I said it, but I wasn't living it. Sometimes you know something is true before you are ready to live by it.

When my mom found out about it all, she reached out to a Jewish organization I had started getting involved with. In a very classic *Sephardi*-mom way, she asked them to help me. No matter what, my mom has always been there for me. She never gave up on me. When I wasn't ready to hear her, she made sure I was surrounded by people who could reach me in a different way.

When October 7th happened, after seeing what was done to my people, something in me broke, and I finally spoke up. I lost thousands of followers on my social media platforms and I understood what antisemitism looks like up close. I received hate I never imagined. I walked into class and saw the same narrative everywhere, even from people I thought were close to me. For the first time, I stopped and asked myself honestly what I was living for.

Around that time, my lease ended, and I had nowhere to go. I found myself in Melbourne and began going to a local *Chabad*. Even in that short window, something in me started to open—a gentle re-entry into a world I had spent years running from.

Choosing *Torah*, This Time for Real

I remember sitting with the *rebbetzin*, her kids climbing all over her, and she answered my questions calmly. Watching her was powerful. The *rabbi* and *rebbetzin* really took me in.

And once I get into something, I go all in. I want to understand it deeply. So that's what I did.

I started praying each morning and began embracing a religious life again, this time because I chose it. I chose *H-shem*, *Torah*, and the beauty of *mitzvot*.

Eventually, I was encouraged to join a program that was originally meant to be in Israel. Because of October 7th, it took place instead in New York, in the Five Towns.

It was incredible to be surrounded by people who genuinely wanted to learn. For me, it wasn't that I suddenly changed overnight. It was more like everything I had been feeling and questioning finally had a place to land. That experience grounded everything. That's when I started keeping *Shabbat*, not out of pressure, but because it made sense.

After the program, I returned to Melbourne and moved into a seminary run by *rebbetzin* Nicole Kornhauser. I remember telling her very clearly, "Listen, when I go out, like to university, I'm going to wear pants. And then I'll put a skirt on when I come back. I'll respect the house, but I'm not going to force myself to become someone I'm not ready to be yet."

That was a very important part of my process. I wanted to take things slowly so that I could actually sustain it, so I took it step by step. I stayed honest about where I was holding, even when it didn't look perfect.

This whole process has been a major transition. Everything in my life shifted, and at first, that was scary. But what I've learned is this: right now, you might feel unsettled by the idea of change. You might feel uncomfortable imagining who you could become. But your future self, the version of you who has made those changes, is at peace with it. So often, we worry about something that, one day, will actually feel completely natural to us. My relationship with *H-shem* deepened, but it also became something more. It became a responsibility.

I think there's a real gap in the Jewish world, especially for people at the beginning of their journey, or even for those who grew up religious. Sometimes people go to *shul* and don't actually know what they're doing. I can read Hebrew, I can figure things out, but there are still moments when I don't know when to stand, when to sit, or what to do. And that's okay.

The transition from being more secular to becoming more observant came with a deeper understanding of my purpose. It brought me clarity, not just spiritually, but practically, even in my career. Now I work for a Jewish organization in New York, where we create elevated events for people who may have had some exposure to Judaism but want to explore it more deeply, in a way that feels relevant and accessible.

When Music Becomes Something More

I love music. I love singing. From my perspective, especially being involved in the music world right now, I see something powerful happening. Jewish women's music is on the rise. There's a real movement happening.

For a long time, many of these spaces were more visible for men, and that's great. But now it's time for women to step into that space as well, to create, perform, and be seen. And I think the key is not just inspiration. It's action.

We need more events for women. More performances. More spaces that are interactive, in-person, real. When I'm on stage singing Hebrew songs, something shifts. I feel connected to something deeper. I'm fully present. And people feel it.

After one performance, a girl came up to me. She told me one of the songs I sang was her father's favorite, and that he had passed away. She was crying. We didn't talk much. We just stood there, holding each other.

That moment stayed with me. You never know how something you create will reach someone. And that's when I understood something bigger. This isn't just about expression. It's about purpose.

Rabbi Shimon's Message: Keeping the Fire Alive

I feel drawn to the ideas of *gilgulim* and *tikkun*. The thought that we come into this world with lifetimes behind us, and that we are here to grow, to repair, and to complete something. I don't fully understand it, but it speaks to me.

There is a teaching that on *Lag BaOmer*, we celebrate *Rabbi Shimon bar Yochai*'s passing with joy, not mourning. *Lag BaOmer*, the day of his passing, is understood as a moment of fulfillment, when he revealed deep *Torah* and completed his mission.

That idea stays with me: live in a way where you use what you were given, where you create something real, and where you leave something behind.

I'm still on that journey. Still growing. Still becoming. And I'm doing it one step at a time.

But now, when someone asks me, "Where are you from? For real?" I don't feel afraid anymore. Because now, I'm living the answer.

Maskit Mati (b. 2003, Israel) is a singer, filmmaker, and writer. Having lived in Israel, Australia, and the United States, her journey shapes her creative voice. She is currently Marketing Manager at Kii NYC, where she creates meaningful, elevated experiences for those exploring Jewish life and identity.

 **maskitmati.enquiries@gmail.com**

@maskitmati

Let Go and Let H–shem: Rebuilding After Loss

BY: NATHALIE LEVY RIESS

I always heard, "You're so strong." Now, I know it. I'm definitely a strong woman, with deep faith and connection. Nothing has shaken that, and now I can say that probably nothing will.

One of the *tefillot* I say with the most *kavanah* in the morning is the one that gives strength to the tired.

It was very challenging to raise nine children, so close together; financially, emotionally, and without a real support system. Being in Israel and adapting to a completely different way of life was challenging in itself. Each of my children, thank G-d, is a powerhouse in his or her own right, so raising smart, deep thinkers is not simple.

At times it really felt like sailing in a rocky boat. I didn't know how I would do it, but I did it. We did it. At the *Pesach* table my children said, "Mom, we should not take for granted anything about our life. It is really a miracle, after all that we've endured, that we can sit in this apartment, and continue to go through it together." We are all in awe, with deep thanks to *H-shem*, that we can see beyond the curtain, knowing there is a plan. There has to be a plan.

In memory of Rabbi Eyal Riess z"l

A Life Built on Faith and Search

I come from Venezuela, and I was always the girl they called the dreamer, the spacey one, because I was always searching for meaning. It didn't make sense to me that this was all that life is about. I always wanted to understand what was behind the scenes. My parents are from Spanish-Moroccan roots, so I grew up with tradition, but without a real understanding of what we were doing. It was just, "That's how Grandma did it. That's how we do it." When I started asking why, there were no answers.

At 18, I traveled to New York as a tourist, and I had a life-changing encounter with the Lubavitcher *Rebbe*, face to face, where literally my spiritual DNA was changed. That's how I describe it, because there was a before and after.

I was enchanted by what I was seeing and feeling. And when I get curious, I go deep. I said, I want to stay here and learn.

I went to one class in Machon Chana, a class in *Tanya* (*Chabad chasidut*). I didn't understand a word, but I understood everything. I stayed there for a year and four months. I quit my plans. I told my parents I was staying in Crown Heights. I ended the relationship I was in. I took on *Shabbat*, *tzniut*, *kashrut*, everything, and it felt completely organic. When the student is ready, the teacher appears, and thank G-d, it was an amazing teacher.

After a full year, I was offered a *shidduch*. I was 19 and a half. Marriage? Who thinks of marriage at that age? And with a stranger? All I knew was that I didn't want an Israeli. And I found out later that he only wanted an Israeli girl. But then we met, and it felt right. We met six times. Eyal was from Tel Aviv, *alav hashalom*. He had also become committed to *Torah u'mitzvot* at the same time as me, in Tzfat. On the sixth date, he proposed. We wrote to the Rebbe, and right away we received an answer. We married four months later.

Nine months later, we had our first child. And then, *baruch H-shem*, eight more came.

Eyal z"l was always a very strong man. Extremely strong, charismatic, a real powerhouse. He built the Tzfat *Kabbalah* Center with his own hands and vision. We used to receive up to 22,000 people a year for programs, touring, *Shabbatons*, and meals at our home. Our home in Tzfat became an open home, with guests every *Shabbat*. It was successful for 20 years, and we built friendships and connections for a lifetime.

When Everything Shifts

And then things began to shift. There were many sources of stress. War. No tourism in Tzfat. Financial pressure. Health challenges in the family. Anxiety. Responsibility. A constant weight. And unfortunately, he developed a very difficult illness, depression. Silent depression.

And one morning, I found him.

It was devastating. I understand now what Aharon felt in that moment, when Moshe spoke to him after the loss of Nadav and Avihu, sharing what *H-shem* had said, that through those who are closest to Him, He is sanctified, and Aharon was silent.

This is the first time I am speaking about it publicly, but I believe in the power of speaking for healing. Men often feel they need to hold everything together, to be strong, to provide, to carry the family. But they are human. They also carry pain, trauma, and pressure.

There is no shame in asking for help. But it has to be the right help. When someone is struggling deeply, especially with thoughts of harming themselves, they need real, professional support, trained, clinical care. Not just someone to speak to casually.

The real tragedy occurs when people feel they cannot ask for that help. My intention in sharing this is to bring awareness.

Living With Grief, Not Against It

It's still painful, still emotional, still very fresh, not even a year. And it's not something that ever feels finished. It is an ongoing journey.

There are days that I'm angry. There are days I ask, haven't I gone through enough? And then I take it to another level and I say, *H-shem*, You trust my strength. So give me a glimpse of what You see in me. Help me understand and feel the strength You know I have.

That strength comes from understanding that this is a journey. I honor each day as it comes. If I need to cry, I cry. If I need to be angry, I allow it. I sit in the pain and in the anger. I allow my children to feel as well, to be angry, to be sad, to have days where they do nothing. This is something you learn to live with.

Grief is as deep as the love was. He was my first love. The memories, the loss, the hollow space, will always be there. You cannot medicate it away. You cannot binge it away. You cannot sleep it away. It becomes part of your life, and you learn to build a new life with it beside you.

The pain shifts. It moves from deep sorrow into something you carry, something you even cherish, even as you miss it. And there are days when the missing physically hurts.

If I could give advice in the midst of tragedy, pain, and loss, it would be this: bring yourself back to the present. Don't let your mind pull you into fear or make things worse than they already are. Being present is painful, but in a place of total loss, there is no other way.

I believe in honesty and vulnerability, but I don't think your children need to see you breaking down. You need to create your own space for that. Then you dry your tears, lift your chin, and go out and be there for them. It's not about pretending or putting on a facade. They need you strong. They are carrying their own pain, their own confusion, their own questions. They need space to feel, to process, to be held, not to become the ones holding us.

Right now, you have to rebuild. There is debris all around you. What is left? What do I have left in me? Take that, and hold onto it for dear life, because your life depends on it.

In Judaism, we are always moving toward rebuilding. I once took a coaching course where they asked what kind of "animal" I had become after everything I had gone through. Our animal soul, the part of us that holds our instincts and strength affects how we respond to life.

And I said, I don't think I became anything. I was always a phoenix. Now I'm simply living it. I am always rebuilding from the ashes, from whatever life brings.

As emotional as things feel, there are moments when you must become practical. What is real right now? What is the next small step? Sometimes that is all you can do.

It's like driving on a dark, rainy night. Your headlights don't show you the whole road. You only see one meter ahead. So you keep going. One meter, then the next, then the next. That is how you move through deep pain. One step at a time. One minute. One hour.

Even during the *shiva*, I said, I am still curious to see what *H-shem* has in store for me. Because if He brought me here, it cannot be just for this. There must be something more for me, for my children, and for the world.

People ask me if I still believe everything *H-shem* does is for the good. And the truth is — I don't define good the way I used to. We think good is what feels good. But life is much bigger than that. Like surgery — it looks painful, but it heals. Like childbirth — it looks chaotic, but it brings life. So I don't pretend to understand. But I stay open. Pain is not just for pain. It has to lead somewhere. I don't know where yet. But I pray, show me Your goodness. Help me see it.

Twenty-six years ago, I experienced something that built that trust. Two of my children became seriously ill at the same time. I had five children under seven. The fear and helplessness were overwhelming. One night, I had a dream. The *Rebbe* came into my kitchen, rinsed the milk utensils, dried his hands, and told me, "Never cut a cake baked in a meat oven with a milk knife."

Then I asked for a blessing. He waved his hand and said, "All is viral." Shortly after, both children recovered fully. It felt like an open miracle, and that experience stayed with me. It became part of my *bitachon*.

MAKING H-SHEM YOURS

Torah has carried me through this. My *emunah* and *bitachon* have only deepened. As a grief coach, everything now feels different, more real, more embodied. I have experienced the infinite wisdom within *shiva*, *shloshim*, and *kaddish*. These are not just traditions. They are a structure that holds you when you cannot hold yourself. I have felt the power of community, the quiet strength of friends who show up, who sit with you, who carry you when you cannot stand on your own. And in the most personal spaces, *hitbodedut*, *tefillah*, and journaling have become my *ir miklat*, my place of refuge.

One of the things I always taught my children is that we must make *H-shem* our own personal *H-shem*. Yes, He is the G-d of *Avraham, Yitzchak, Yaakov, Sarah, Rivka, Rachel, Leah, Yosef, Moshe*, and all the giants who came before us. But *Shavuot* is not only about giving the *Torah*. It is about receiving it, making it yours. Living it. Letting it enter your life in a real and personal way. Because at the end of the day, *H-shem hu Elokecha*. He is your G-d. Make that relationship personal.

Don't stop asking. Don't stop learning. Life is much bigger than what we see. *Torah* is deep, eternal, infinite. You can always approach it in a new way. Bring *H-shem* into who you are. Don't leave yourself behind to meet Him. If you love singing, sing. If you love writing, write. If you love teaching, teach. Follow that pull. It was given to you because it is part of your purpose. Part of your light.

So I wish for anyone going through a challenge that they find the strength within themselves, and bring it out in the best way.

Even without all the answers.

Even without full understanding.

Still choosing to continue.

Nathalie Levy Riess is a NLP Master, emotional trauma and grief therapist, family systems therapist, Kabbalah mentor, teacher, and motivational speaker. Director of the Tzfat Kabbalah Center. Currently living in Ra'anana, Israel with her younger children.
Nathalieriess@gmail.com

MITZVAH IN THE SPOTLIGHT: NETILAT YADAYIM

Sanctifying Our Hands, Elevating Our Lives

BY: ORLY WAHBA

There are *mitzvot* we struggle to take on. And then there are *mitzvot* we think we already understand. *Netilat yadayim* was always one of those for me.

I love eating bread. I genuinely cannot start my day without it. And for me, it's not just about the food — it's about what comes with it. The pause. The washing. Sitting down properly. *Birkat Hamazon*, which carries such a powerful *segulah* for *parnassa*. I know it could be much more comfortable to reach for something quick just to avoid the length of *Birkat Hamazon*. But washing and *Birkat Hamazon* are not interruptions to the day. They are the strongest way to begin it. They set the tone. They open the flow. They align you with *bracha* before anything else even starts.

Netilat yadayim itself became something I moved through quickly. I poured, I dried, and I continued. Until I stopped and asked myself a question that shifted everything: What am I actually doing?

Because if *H-shem* gave us a *mitzvah* that we repeat multiple times a day, it cannot be meant to live on autopilot. The truth is, we often lose the value of what we are doing. We rush through it, we check it off, and we move on. But it is not the action alone that elevates a *mitzvah*. It is the *kavana* we bring into it.

A few years ago, right before I came to Israel, my cousin called me. He was going through a very real struggle with *parnassa*, hitting wall after wall, and he went to his *rav* asking for guidance. The answer he received was simple, almost disarmingly so: to do *netilat yadayim* with copper. He told me, "I already do *netilat yadayim*. What does copper have to do with anything?"

He tried to find a copper cup and couldn't, so he made one himself and began asking deeper questions. Why copper? What is the connection?

We know that *netilat yadayim* can be performed with any proper vessel, so what is really happening here beneath the surface? Sources from *Torah*, from *Kabbalah*, patterns that repeat themselves — all pointing to the fact that this *mitzvah* is far more powerful than we tend to experience it.

When he called me back, he didn't talk about a product. He said, "We need to bring this back to *Am Yisrael*." And in that moment, it became clear to me that this was not something I could turn away from.

Today, those same copper cups — once suggested quietly by a *rav* — are placed at the *Kotel*, used by millions, standing there as a reminder of what once was and what will be again. Waiting, in a sense, for the day when the *Beit Hamikdash* will be rebuilt, and the *kohanim* will return to their service, washing their hands once more from copper, just as they did before.

At its core, this *mitzvah* lives in the world of *asiyah* — action. Judaism is not only about what we think or feel; it is defined by what we do. And everything we bring into this world ultimately passes through our hands.

They build, give, create, and sustain. They are the place where intention becomes reality. So when our hands are purified, we are not performing a symbolic act. We are refining the very *kli* through which our lives take shape.

And this is also why the *mitzvah* is not performed directly from the sink. Because this is not simply about water reaching the hands. It is about taking an action and giving it form. A *kli* transforms the act into something intentional — it defines it, contains it, and elevates it from a physical motion into a conscious *mitzvah*.

But here is where most of us miss it. We rush the filling of the cup, when we are meant to fill it fully. We let the water barely touch our hands, when it is meant to reach the wrist. We say the *bracha* quickly, sometimes even after drying, disconnecting the blessing from the act itself. And then we wonder why it feels empty. The shift is not complicated. It is a matter of presence.

The idea of copper added another dimension that I could not ignore. In the *Mishkan*, when *H-shem* commands Moshe to build the *kiyor*, the basin from which the *kohanim* would wash before performing the holiest service, it is made specifically from copper. Not gold, not silver — copper. And even more striking, it was made from the mirrors of the women in *Mitzrayim* — women who, in the darkest reality, chose to build life, to restore connection, and to ensure continuity. Those mirrors, objects of reflection and physicality, became a *kli* of sanctification.

There is also a teaching that compares copper to *Am Yisrael*. Copper darkens over time; it loses its shine. And yet, it can be restored — cleaned, renewed, brought back to its original brightness with remarkable ease. That is *teshuvah*.

The *kohanim* did not begin their service without washing their hands, not because they were dirty, but because they were about to do something meaningful. And that is the point. Our lives are not separate from that model. Our homes are our *Mishkan*, our actions are our service, and *netilat yadayim* is the moment we choose how we enter into them.

There is no need to approach this with overwhelm. If this is not yet part of your life, begin with one moment. If it already is, go deeper, not wider. Slow it down. Be present. Add intention. Because the power of this *mitzvah* is not in how much we do, but in how aware we are when we do it. It takes less than a minute. And yet, that minute has the ability to shape everything that follows.

Orly Wahba is a passionate educator, speaker, and licensed Israeli tour guide based in Jerusalem. She is the founder of Abraham's Legacy, a global *Tehillim* platform, and *Netillah*, a 100% pure copper washing cup initiative. Through *Tanach*, history, and faith, she inspires connection, unity, and meaningful daily living.

▶ **info@netillah.com**

🌐 **Apply 10% Off at netillah.com/ coupons/her-tribe**

Rabbanit Rachel Bazak

Receiving the Torah – As Women, As a Generation

IN LIGHT OF
RABBI MORDECHAI ELIYAHU ZT"L,
THE GRANDFATHER
OF *RABBANIT* RACHEL BAZAK

What is your biggest dream when it comes to your *shlichut* and your impact on women?

The great dream of my *neshama* is that every Jewish woman and girl in the world will feel a deep closeness to *H-shem* — not only as an idea, but as a lived experience — and will merit to live a life of holiness according to *halacha* and according to Kabbalah.

I grew up in the path of my holy grandfather, and I saw with my own eyes a way of living where *halacha* is aligned with the inner dimension. The actions and the soul move together.

I saw how much light there is in this path. How much honor there is for a woman, for every person. How much warmth, how much pleasantness.

And I want to help people live this way. Because I see how much pain there is in the world, especially among women and girls. I believe that when a person lives aligned with *Torah*, life becomes filled with light, joy, and love. And that is what every soul truly seeks. This is the path I was shown, and I pray to merit to make it accessible to all hearts.

Geulah feels very close today. How can we live with that awareness, with calm and emunah?

It is a very beautiful question. *H-shem* loves us very much. I feel that we are already in *Geulah*. I feel that we are in a birth — a birth of a nation, a birth of a new spiritual level. And in birth, there is pressure. There is crying. There is pain. But it is still a birth. When I hold that awareness — that I am inside a birth — I receive the strength to carry the process.

And this is what is happening to us now. There is pressure, there is pain, but we are in a birth. We are in *Geulah*. And *H-shem* loves us with an eternal love.

One day, our eyes will open and we will understand everything. Why souls came. Why souls left. We will see the full picture and understand how it was all love, compassion, and kindness.

What does Geulah mean in everyday life?

It means to live with a kind of double vision. Not only to see with physical eyes, but also to see the Divine within everything. There is a sentence that accompanies me daily: "everything is *beseder*" — there is Divine order, everything is *beseder Eloki*.

This reaches even the smallest details. When something feels wrong, I remind myself: nothing is broken. There is order here. Everything is guided. Everything is blessed. You are protected. You are surrounded.

Thanks to this perspective, my life becomes calmer. I feel more joy, *Baruch Hashem*. I plan my day, but I leave space for the Divine order. I say: *H-shem*, bless this day. And inside, I stay flexible, soft, and open to what unfolds. Since the light is always moving, plans often change. So I tell myself not to try to control everything. I am gentle with myself, and gentle with others. In every moment, new light enters, and reality is created again.

What is the deeper essence of Matan Torah?

Matan Torah is the wedding. It is unification with *H-shem*.

Am Yisrael, *H-shem*, and the *Torah* are one. These days, I feel that this awareness is expanding — and it heals so much of the anxiety and pain that exists in the world. For fear comes from separation. From feeling that there is "me" and there is *H-shem*. But when we are one, when He is revealed within us — that is *Geulah*. *Matan Torah* is love. Love in *gematria* is *echad* — oneness. And the *Torah* is one with *H-shem*.

For example, when you read a poem, you meet the soul of the poet. So too, when you learn *Torah*, you meet the soul of the Infinite. The *Baal Shem Tov* teaches that every word, every letter in the *Torah*, is like entering a room filled with light. *Matan Torah* is this meeting with the Infinite. There are no words to describe this unity.

What is the message of Megillat Ruth for women today?

I love *Ruth*, the mother of royalty.

I imagine her sitting near *King Shlomo*, as the *Midrash* says. She merited a long life and saw generations. And I think about the power of one woman who brought royalty to *Am Yisrael*.

Such humility. She did not place herself at the center. She followed. She listened. She built. She focused on building the house of Yisrael. My grandfather told me that women will bring the *Geulah*, through feminine wisdom, feminine courage, and openness.

A woman has within her a space where new life is created. This is the gateway to *Geulah*. Every woman must understand how essential she is. How much the world depends on her. Her courage together with her humility, her strength together with her softness — this is what will bring *Geulah*.

How can women build unity without ego or competition?

First, you must know that no one can take what belongs to you. The souls you are meant to influence belong to you. Your place in the world is yours alone. And I have seen that when we connect with one another, it multiplies our strength.

Unity increases light. I learned this from my father. He constantly elevates others. He makes people around him greater, and it does not make him smaller. Because when you elevate others, you increase the light of *H-shem* in the world. And our souls become united.

What should a woman focus on before Shavuot?

To become humble. *Malchut* is humility — it has nothing of its own. And this state allows light to enter. It is not always easy, because before humility, there can be a feeling of breaking — as if something you held onto is falling apart. And then you say: I agree. I agree not to know. This openness creates a vessel. A vessel to receive *Torah*.

In the Torah, women play central roles, yet today their spiritual space sometimes seems less visible. What is the correct way to understand a woman's role?

The *Arizal* writes that in the generation of redemption, the souls of figures from *Tanach* become interwoven within our souls.

Today, we see this in new forms. Women carry so much. They learn *Torah*, they build homes, they provide, they raise families. This is not less than the past. They have the same essence, expressed in the clothing of today. And I believe this essence will continue to grow and change.

The more women are connected to *H-shem*, the more they will step into meaningful roles, and the process of redemption will move forward. Because when a woman is a *yirat Shamayim*, she places *H-shem* at the center — and through her, *Am Yisrael* advances.

What is your guidance for women seeking a zivug, and for those who are married?

For women seeking a mate:

Before meeting someone, there is a *segulah* my grandfather taught — to open *Tehillim* to any chapter, read ten chapters, and say: "bring the good closer and distance the bad."

When you come from a place of *tefillah*, you arrive with clarity. Also, I believe that one should allow the dating process to unfold slowly and not to rush the process. A true connection develops over time. Sometimes it may not yet reveal itself fully at the onset and may require more time to develop. Give it space. There is a soul-dance that needs time to be revealed and developed.

For married women:

Return to softness. Life requires strength, but sometimes we bring too much strength into the relationship with our spouse. A man needs gentleness, presence and admiration. And this does not make a woman smaller. It builds something beautiful in the home.

At the same time, there must also be boundaries, together with warmth, respect, and an *ayin tova*–positivity.

And from the side of the mother-in-law: Ask your daughter-in-law: What would make you feel good? How can I support you?

Because what we think is helpful is not always what the other needs. When a person feels valued, it heals the relationship. When a person feels seen for her soul — not only her shortcomings — healing comes. It always comes.

*B*lessing
I bless all the women reading this, that you should merit to come to *Eretz Yisrael*, to the *Beit HaMikdash*, to hear the singing of the *Leviim*, and to be among the women who bring the *Geulah*. *Amen*.

[Special Thank you to Keren Miller for translation from Hebrew to English]

Rabbanit Rachel Bazak is a dedicated teacher and spiritual guide, deeply influenced by her grandfather, *Rabbi Mordechai Eliyahu zt"l*. Through her work, she brings women closer to *H-shem* and to the depth of *Torah*, weaving together faith, tradition, and personal growth with warmth, clarity, and a strong commitment to authentic Jewish living.

For lectures and events:
Benayahu +972 054 815 19 49

*W*hat can we learn from *Naomi* and *Ruth* about the relationship between mother-in-law and daughter-in-law?
Ruth respected *Naomi* deeply, like a mother. This is the key in such relationships.

Ask yourself: if this were my mother, how would I respond to her?

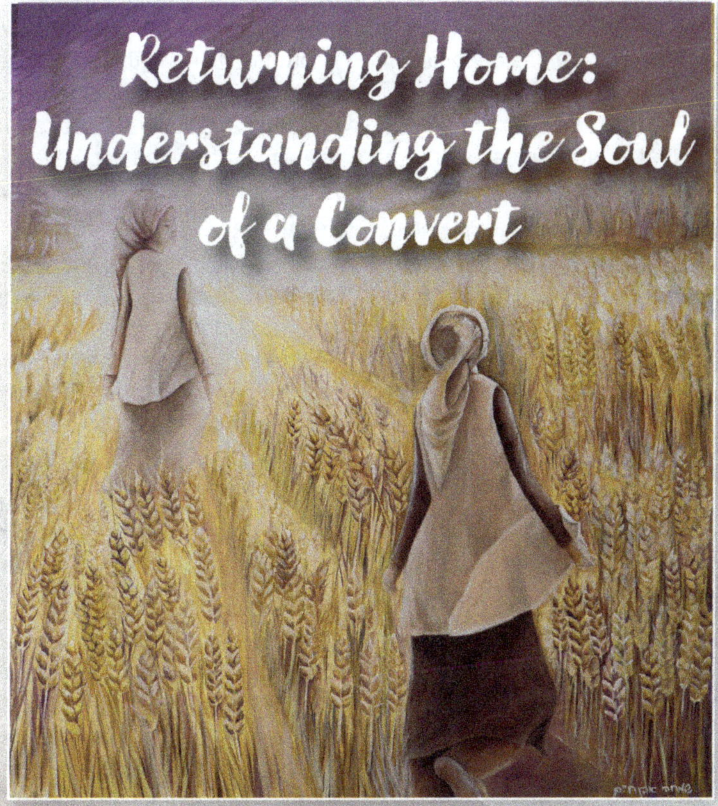

SIMCHA EVEN CHAIMI RUTH AND NAOMI I SIMCHA-ART.CO.IL

BY: RIVKA MALKA PERLMAN

"What if the people we see as newcomers are actually carrying the deepest roots of who we are?"

As Shavuot approaches, we prepare to celebrate receiving the *Torah*. On this holiday, we read the story of *Ruth*, a convert, and the life she lived.

One of the reasons we read *The Book of Ruth* is because, in a certain sense, we all started out as converts. Before we received the *Torah*, we were just a family. Then we stood at *Har Sinai*, accepted it, and entered into something new. Her story parallels ours more than we realize.

When I was growing up, I knew one person who had converted to Judaism. Today, I have friends, teachers, and women in my community. So many of them are converts. It is remarkable how much the landscape has changed. People say this everywhere. Something is happening in the world. *Geula* is truly unfolding. Souls are returning to their rightful places. New souls that we need are coming down.

We speak about converts even in our daily prayers. We ask to be connected with the righteous convert. We say, "Place us with them." We want to be aligned with that level of sincerity and purity. It is a *mitzvah* to love a convert.

But we have to ask ourselves honestly: Do converts feel loved, or do they still feel more like newcomers?

There is a profound teaching brought in the *Zohar* that shifts how we understand souls, birth, and the journey of those who come home to the Jewish people. When a husband and wife bring a child into the world, their union draws down a soul into a body. This is the natural order. But when *tzaddikim* bring children into the world, something greater is set in motion. Their spiritual union does not generate only the soul that enters the child. It produces an overflow, additional souls, luminous and unassigned. These souls do not disappear. They become light.

The *Zohar* teaches that when a person chooses to convert, a soul from this elevated realm is sent down. It descends from beneath the *Shechinah*, embraced before entering the body.

This is not a simple beginning. It is a return. These are not ordinary souls. They are souls that were always meant to arrive, souls that carry a certain light, something that can often be felt even before the journey is complete. These are souls prepared long before, rooted in something higher, now finding their place within the Jewish people.

If that is true, then everything about how we see converts needs to shift. They are not arriving empty. They are arriving with something.

This is why the story of *Ruth* is central to our tradition. *Ruth* had once been a princess. Then her life unraveled. Her husband and children died, and she was left with nothing, no security, no future, no reason to stay. She could have gone back. She had every reason to.

But there was *Naomi*, her mother-in-law, who also had nothing left. *Ruth* looked at her and realized something very simple. She had nothing to give. She could not offer children, security, or comfort in any conventional way. So she made a different choice.

"I have nothing to give you, so I will give you myself." She did not offer solutions. She offered presence. "Where you go, I will go. What you need, I will get you. I am here."

She was not looking for another life or another opportunity. She chose responsibility, connection, and kindness. *Ruth* did not simply perform acts of kindness. She became a source of it. She brought kindness back to the Jewish people not because of what she had, but because of who she chose to become. From her came *King David*, and ultimately *Mashiach*, the future of the Jewish people.

The *Torah* was given in the desert, a place that is open, simple, and humble. To receive it, we have to become like that space. Less certain. More open. Willing to receive. This is what converts live. Notice the greatness in people who have converted to Judaism, or in anyone who has walked a difficult road. Step down a little. Approach with more humility and begin to understand how much we can learn from one another, and how much we can learn from them.

In that space, we begin to resemble *Har Sinai* itself, simple and unassuming, yet ready to receive, ready to shine with blooming flowers and a kind of beauty that comes from loving one another and being truly non-judgmental. And then take it one step further and make it real.

You can say something simple: "I never really thought about what it took to get here. If you are open to sharing, I would love to hear a little about your journey." And if they do not want to share, that is okay. Think well of them. Send a blessing. Ask *H-shem* to look out for them. Recognize that they are carrying something special. And then ask yourself:

How can I grow from this? How can I become a little more like that? Because in the end, this is not just about how we see them. It is about who we choose to become.

Rivka Malka Perlman is a Jewish Educator and founder of The Redemption School for Coaching and Transformation. Her mission is to guide women through uncharted territory to a celebration of their connection to themselves, to each other and to G-d. She coaches, teaches and leads the Redemption Retreat.

🌐 **rivkamalka.com**

▶ **theredemptionschool@gmail.com**

RABBANIT CHANA HENKIN:

FROM RUTH TO TODAY'S NASHIM TZIDKANIOT

CHOOSING, RECEIVING, AND LIVING TORAH ACROSS GENERATIONS

There are women whose presence feels like a bridge between generations, between tradition and lived life, between what came before and what continues to unfold. In this conversation, we meet *Rabbanit* Chana Henkin, founder and chancellor of the *Nishmat* Women's Program, to explore women in *Tanach*, our roles today, and how text-based learning helps us draw closer to *Torah* and enrich our lives. Whatever our life stage, we are invited to engage, to receive *Torah*, and to let it strengthen our connection to *H-shem*, ourselves, our family and our community.

Editorial Disclaimer:
Yoatzot Halacha do not serve as rabbis or assume rabbinic roles. Rather, they offer women-to-women guidance in taharat hamishapcha and women's health, within established halachic frameworks—enhancing accessibility and understanding of Jewish law, while remaining fully aligned with Orthodox tradition.

Q: PLEASE TELL US ABOUT YOUR PERSONAL JOURNEY AND WHAT LED YOU TO WOMEN'S *TORAH* LEADERSHIP?

My parents were part of that immigrant generation in the United States before there were *yeshivot*. But religion was paramount in our home, and my parents were passionate about their children's *Torah* education. *Torah* was palpable, and the warmth of Judaism was ever-present.

My mother had several miscarriages before I was born. My much-older brothers taught me to read Hebrew before first grade. When my mother saw that, she said, "If my daughter can learn Hebrew, I can learn too." So my brothers taught her to read, and without understanding word for word, her *shmoneh esreh* would last for 45 minutes every morning! That was formative for me, together with my father's character traits and his love of *davening*. He sang words of *tefillah* constantly.

From the start, as a child, I felt a tremendous thirst for *Torah* learning, but I did not want a mediated experience. I did not want someone to give me conclusions. I wanted to encounter the text myself and feel that *H-shem* is there.

That desire stayed with me. When I began teaching, I understood that there needed to be a *Makom Torah* for women, a *bet midrash* open to all backgrounds. That is what led me and Rav Henkin to establish *Nishmat*.

Q: WAS THERE A MOMENT THAT CLARIFIED YOUR MISSION?

Seven years after *Nishmat* was established, there was a moment of *hashgachah*, Divine guidance. I met a friend one morning who burst into tears because she and her husband were unable to live a normal married life due to *halachic* uncertainty. She had no clear guidance, no accessible address.

I realized this was not just her story. We needed women trained at a high level to guide other women in issues of family purity — *taharat hamishpacha*. That day, I changed my plans, and in 24 hours, a sea-change in Jewish history was underway.

I went to *rabbanim* and to doctors, and began building a program that integrates *halacha* with understanding of the female body.

Today, our *Yoetzot Halacha* have helped women to find answers to hundreds of thousands of questions, and are helping bring Jewish babies into the world. Many women have told me, "This is your baby."

It is not about changing *halacha*. It is about making it accessible with clarity and dignity.

Q: WHAT HAS SURPRISED YOU MOST ALONG THE WAY?

That when women access *Torah* directly, it transforms their relationship with *H-shem*.

PHOTO COURTESY OF NISHMAT

When a woman learns the text with a study partner, it becomes a real encounter. That connection can sustain her through difficult times in life.

Q: WHICH FEMALE FIGURE IN *TANACH* DO YOU FEEL MOST CONNECTED TO?

At this time of year, *Ruth*. She begins as an outsider and becomes someone who shapes the future of *Am Yisrael*. But if you met her, she would insist that she was an ordinary woman.

That is the point. Ordinary people can achieve greatness.

For many years, I believed someone great would create a place for women's *Torah* learning at the highest level. Then I realized that if no one else is doing it, I will have to do it.

Q: MANY WOMEN FEEL OVERWHELMED APPROACHING *TORAH* LEARNING. HOW WOULD YOU GUIDE THEM?

Many women approach *Torah* like a child in a toy store. Everything is exciting and everything pulls you in.

But you cannot grow that way or learn everything in one day.

Choose one area. Break it into small pieces. Learn consistently. Over time, you will see what you have built.

Torah is not only intellectual. It is a meeting with *H-shem*. It requires patience and structure.

Q: WHAT ABOUT WOMEN WHO FEEL THEY SIMPLY DO NOT HAVE TIME?

Women are busy with children, work, and responsibilities. That is real.

But *Torah* does not have to be separate from life. Bring your learning into your life, into your home, into your *Shabbat* table, and into your conversations with your children.

Even something small can have a deep impact.

My husband was very much influenced by his mother and his grandmother. He dedicated much of his life to helping women and he was a central address for women's *halachic* questions. I spent the past year and a half translating into English and publishing his Responsa spanning four decades of questions he received from women, "*Responsa on Contemporary Jewish Women's Issues*" (available at Ktav.com or Amazon.com). The book focuses on women's *mitzvot*, the synagogue, family, modesty, and more. This became the overarching priority in my life, to enable women to learn these reponsa together, to make our Jewish womanhood more meaningful.

Q: HOW DO YOU BALANCE DEEP *TORAH* LEARNING WITH *TEFILLAH* AND PERSONAL CONNECTION?

There were years when I felt I did not have the energy for *davening Selichot*. I would say I was too tired.

But every time I went to *daven*, I would think, how did I almost miss this?

Tefillah can feel like a burden, but it can also uplift and guide you. The goal is not to remove the effort, but to experience what it gives you.

Q: HOW CAN WOMEN BUILD UNITY WHILE HONORING DIFFERENT LEVELS OF OBSERVANCE?

Nothing beats learning together. When you place a text in front of a group of women, each brings her own perspective and insight. Suddenly, there's a sense of sisterhood.

You do not weaken your own commitment. You deepen it, while appreciating what others bring.

That is how we build real *Ahavat Yisrael.*

Q: WHAT ADVICE WOULD YOU GIVE WOMEN LEADING *TORAH* STUDY CIRCLES?

Do not see yourself as someone giving over information. Create a space where you are learning together.

Base it on a text. Build incrementally. Let each session grow from the previous one.

When women are active participants, not passive listeners, the experience becomes empowering and sustainable.

Q: WHAT IS THE CENTRAL MESSAGE OF *SHAVUOT* FOR WOMEN TODAY?

Shavuot is unique. There is no single defining *mitzvah* like *matzah* or *shofar.*

H-shem gave the *Torah* once, but receiving the *Torah* happens every day.

The *mitzvah* of *Shavuot* is learning *Torah*, especially through effort, staying up, pushing beyond comfort. There is something powerful in that experience. You feel the Divine Presence.

The reward for you and your family is immense.

Q: WHAT IS ONE MESSAGE YOU WOULD LIKE WOMEN TO CARRY WITH THEM?

You do not need to be extraordinary to impact Jewish life.

Ordinary women can achieve extraordinary things.

And that is the essence of *Shavuot*, to choose *Torah* again and again.

Rabbanit Chana Henkin has transformed women's *Torah* scholarship and leadership, including establishing *Nishmat's* revolutionary *Yoetzet Halacha* program. She made *aliyah* in 1972 with her husband, the esteemed *posek* Rabbi Yehuda Henkin *ztz"l*. They have six children, including Rav Eitam and Naama Henkin, murdered by Hamas terrorists in 2015, and many grandchildren. Join the *Nishmat* Summer Program:

🌐 **Nishmat.net/ summer-beit-midrash**

JUNE 28–JULY 16, 2026

Text-based, in-depth learning with top Torah educators in Jerusalem

Choose from 3 levels of classes suited to all learning backgrounds

Hear from world-renowned guest speakers from across the Jewish world

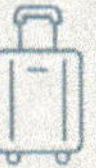
Join for 1, 2 or 3 weeks, depending on your availability

For details and registration, visit
nishmat.net/summer-beit-midrash
or scan the QR code on the right

HOW TO ADD THE "ALWAYS"

INTO "PUTTING H-SHEM BEFORE ME"

BY: SARA YOHEVED RIGLER

Our problem is not that we don't believe. Our problem is that we don't remember.

On that very first *Shavuos*, 3338 years ago, when *H-shem* introduced Himself to *Am Yisrael* at *Har Sinai*, He declared: "I am the Lord your *G-d* who took you out of the land of Egypt, out of the house of bondage." According to the Sages, this is the commandment of *Emunah*, the commandment to believe in *G-d*.

The commandment to believe is not like a beautiful glass sculpture you buy and put on a shelf, and from then on, it's yours. Rather, we are enjoined to engage with this *mitzvah*, to be aware of it, to be conscious of it. How often? Constantly.

The *Sefer HaChinuch* points out that the *mitzvahs* apply at particular times and situations except for six *mitzvahs* "whose obligation is constant and does not cease from a person for even one moment of his life." It calls them, "the Six Constant *Mitzvahs*."

Belief in *G-d*, the first of the Ten Commandments, is the first of the Six Constant *Mitzvahs*. But how do we actually fulfill this *mitzvah*? Belief in *G-d* entails believing that *G-d* is the Creator, the Sustainer and the Supervisor of the Universe, as the *Sefer HaChinuch* delineates:

As Creator: He made this world from nothing.

As Sustainer: He continually wills every particle into existence.

As Supervisor: He orchestrates everything that happens to us.

We all *believe* these principles, but do we *remember* them when we're getting dressed? When we're walking from our car to the dentist's office? When we're waiting in line at the supermarket? Our lives are filled with downtime that presents a perfect opportunity to fulfill the *mitzvah d'orraisa* of believing in *H-shem*. But how do we remember?

MY GOAL, EVERY JEW'S GOAL

If I had to name the goal of the fifty years of my spiritual journey, it would be: To be G-d-conscious. As *Dovid HaMelech* put it: "*Shivisi H-shem l'negedi tamid,* I put G-d before me always."

This is not just a personal goal of *Dovid HaMelech* and me. In the *Rama's* very first annotation to the *Shulchan Aruch*, he quotes "*Shivisi Hashem l'negedi tamid,*" and calls it "a major principle in the *Torah*," an assertion the *Chofetz Chaim* repeats on the opening page of the *Mishnah Berurah*.

Yet, for fifty years this goal eluded me. Sure, I remembered *H-shem* when I *dovened*, when I said *brachas* over food (usually), and whenever I really needed something, such as my computer to behave. But when I got into bed at night and was about to say the bedtime *Shema*, I always felt a tinge of surprise, like when one of my grandchildren whom I haven't seen for a while suddenly shows up at my door. Where had *H-shem* been all day as I did the laundry, prepared lunch for my

husband, worked on my latest book, or walked in the park for exercise?

Then, a couple years ago, I discovered the teachings of Rabbi Asher Boruch Wegbreit and his program of what he calls, "KLM, *Kavanah L' Mitzvos*." His idea was simple, but life-transforming. I can turn all of my mundane activities into *mitzvahs* simply by having the *kavanah* that what I am about to do is a *mitzvah* commanded by *H-shem*. Doing the laundry? The *mitzvah* of *chesed*. Preparing lunch for my husband? The *mitzvah* of *la'leches b'drachav*, emulating *H-shem*, who feeds the whole world. Walking for exercise? The *mitzvah* of *nishmartem me'od l'nafshotechem*, taking very good care of my health. Just by prefacing these actions with mindfulness, with a short statement of *kavanah*, presto! *H-shem* is present.

This practice finally got me within sight of my goal of remembering *H-shem* always. I became so excited about the power of this simple practice that I have written a book about it, "*8 Seconds to Connect with Hashem: Mitzvah Mindfulness for Women*". Through precise lists and stories (my own and other women's), the book shows how to bring *H-shem* into the gym, the kitchen, the workplace, even vacations.

Now when I'm walking to the bus stop, instead of my mind wandering to what I have to do tomorrow or what I should have done yesterday, I fulfill the holy *mitzvah* of believing in *H-shem*. I say, "I am fulfilling the *mitzvah* of knowing there is a *G-d*, as You commanded me, *H-shem*, in order to bond with you." (This takes just 8 seconds.)

Then I am mindful that *H-shem*, the Creator, created my legs that enable me to walk and also created the trees that line the street. Then I am mindful that *H-shem*, the Sustainer, is at this moment willing everything into existence, that He is animating all the cells of my body and all the atoms of the passing cars, the pavement, and the people I pass. Then I am mindful that *H-shem*, the Supervisor, determines everything that happens, whether I'll catch the bus or miss it, whether I'll succeed in finding what I need to buy or not.

I may appear to be walking alone, but by this simple practice of mindfulness, by fulfilling the *mitzvah* of *Emunah*, I am actually walking with *H-shem*.

Sara Yoheved Rigler is a highly acclaimed international lecturer on Jewish spirituality. She has lectured in five continents and over 35 American cities.

Books: *Holy Woman; Battle Plans: How to Fight the Yetzer Hara; Emunah with Love and Chicken Soup; I've Been Here Before: When Souls of the Holocaust Return.*

🌐 **sararigler.com**
🌐 **8secconnect.com**

THE SONG OF THE SOUL:
The Inner Voice of King David

BY: REBBETZIN HANNAH MIRYAM BEJARANO GUTIERREZ

The festival of *Shavuot*, celebrated as *Zeman Matan Torateinu* — "the time of the giving of our *Torah*," is a moment when the soul can ascend to a heightened spiritual elevation. It is a sacred meeting point where Heaven and earth unite through the profound revelation brought by *H-shem*. Yet within this elevated time lies another deeply personal layer, a collective soul memory rooted in the tradition that *King David* was both born and departed from this world on this very day.

This convergence is not coincidental. Through the life of *King David*, we come to understand the essence of the human experience. We are given permission to feel our imperfections and stand authentically before our Creator, while still striving to grow, heal, and draw closer to *H-shem*. Through his poetic gift, *King David* gave voice to the full spectrum of human emotion, revealing both fragility and beauty.

He teaches us that it is okay to be imperfect, to struggle, and even to feel broken at times. The greatness of the human experience is not found in avoiding hardship, but in the courage to bring our inner world before *H-shem* with honesty and vulnerability.

As it says in *Tehillim* 34:2:
"Avarechah et A-onai b'chol et, tamid tehilato b'fi"
"I bless *H-shem* at all times; His praise is always in my mouth."

Tehillim is not only a way to honor *H-shem*. It is the language through which the soul expresses the depth of human experience.

On *Shavuot*, as we stand once again at Sinai to receive the *Torah* anew, we also encounter the soul of *King David*. His life teaches us how to internalize both emotion and *Torah*, how to allow *Torah* to live within us and transform us. He shows us the beauty of becoming a vessel for *H-shem*'s Divine expression. His passing reminds us that a life devoted to *H-shem* leaves an imprint beyond time.

Shavuot thus becomes not only a commemoration of revelation, but also a celebration of the depth and purpose of the human experience. In remembering *King David*, we are encouraged to live with authenticity, connection, and emotional honesty.

It is easy to view *King David* as distant. Yet when we open *Tehillim*, we encounter not only a king chosen by *H-shem*, but a deeply human soul who struggled, felt, and endured.

King David experienced rejection, fear, regret, and brokenness. Yet instead of silencing those emotions, he transformed them into *tefillah*.

One powerful expression of this is:
"Min ha-meitzar karati H-shem"
"From the narrow place, I called out to *H-shem*." (*Tehillim* 118:5)

Who among us does not know that "narrow place"? Moments when emotions feel constricted, when exhaustion weighs heavily; yet we quietly continue caring for others while wondering how we will keep going.

King David teaches us that we do not need to be perfect to connect with *H-shem*. We can bring our struggles, our imperfect hearts, and our raw emotions, and that itself becomes a beautiful *tefillah*.

For Jewish women balancing home, family, *Avodat H-shem*, and personal growth, his message is deeply comforting: your voice matters. Your *tefillah* matters. Your inner world is worthy of being heard.

Tehillim becomes a powerful tool, especially in moments of challenge. Its strength lies in sincerity and consistency.

First, designate a psalm for each emotion. Connection to *H-shem* does not require readiness, only honesty. Choose a perek that reflects your emotional state.

Feeling overwhelmed? Return to *Min ha-meitzar.*

Feeling grateful? Open to *Mizmor le Todah.*

Allow yourself to use the power of *Tehillim* to meet *H-shem* from exactly where you are.

Second, let your soul sing. Even a quiet melody can transform heaviness into lightness.

Ivdu et H-shem b'simchah, "serve *H-shem* with joy."

Third, reflect daily. Choose one *pasuk*, write it down, and sit with it. Let it settle deeply within.

King David's words are eternal. They accompany us through every generation, in struggle and in gratitude.

Our sages teach that *Mashiach* will come from his line. His voice is part of our future.

On *Shavuot*, we remember that *Torah* is meant to be lived. *H-shem* seeks sincerity, not perfection.

Tehillim becomes a bridge between our humanity and the Divine.

As it says:
"*Kol haneshamah tehallel H-shem*," "Let every soul praise *H-shem*."

Each of us carries a *chelek*, a piece of purpose that only we can bring into the world.

And perhaps this is the deepest point: *Torah* is how *H-shem* speaks to us, and *Tehillim* teaches us how to respond.

In this connection between *Shavuot* and *King David*, we are invited to listen inward, to honor our emotions, and to elevate them through *Torah* and *tefillah*. Every whisper of the heart can become a song, and every song can become a bridge to *H-shem*. When we allow ourselves to feel and to speak, we continue the legacy of *King David*, transforming life into *kedushah* and drawing the Divine closer into our daily lives. In doing so, we prepare ourselves to receive the *Torah* not only as a gift, but as a living voice within our souls.

Rebbetzin Hannah Miryam Bejarano Gutierrez is a devoted creator, writer, painter, and autism advocate. She leads Jewish Posh Living Magazine and authored *A Memoir to Human Emotion.* A speaker and coach, she integrates *Torah*-based healing and creativity, inspiring others toward *emunah*, growth, and connection to *H-shem*.

🌐 **contactjewishposhlivingmag@ gmail.com**

▶ **rebbetzinhannahm.wixsite.com/ website**

Download the  **ABRAHAM'S LEGACY** Tehillim App

Just ONE MINUTE a day can help complete a book of Tehillim in minutes with people from around the world.

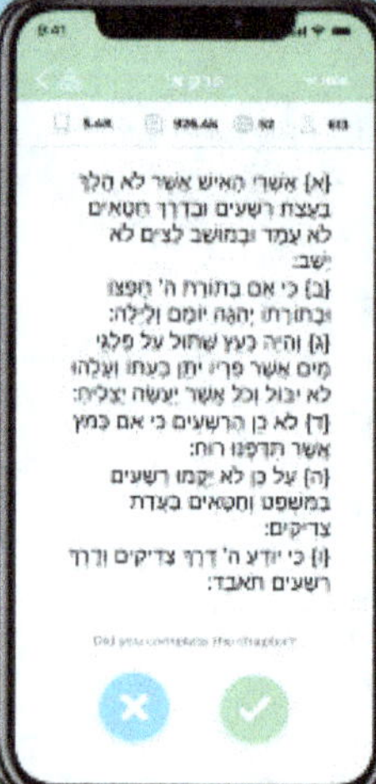

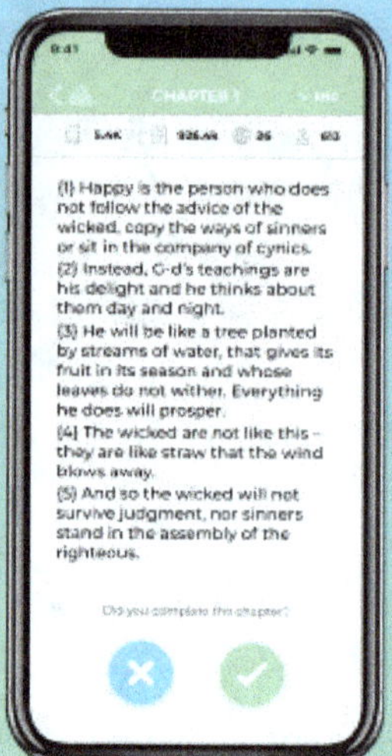

FEATURES INCLUDE :

PRAYER CIRCLES
Create prayer groups with individualized links.

CHAT
Update members about the person for whom you're praying.

VERSES BY NAME
See chapters to read based on a person's name.

REMINDERS
Set daily reminders to pray.

LANGUAGES
Available in Hebrew, English, French, Spanish and Transliteration.

GLOBAL STATS
See chapters and books completed , number of readers, and participating countries.

WHY JOIN?

We turn to Tehillim for blessings, health, parnassah, shidduchim, children, security, and success.
JOIN US.

abrahamslegacy.com

ATARA: Serving H-shem through the Arts

BY: ANNIE ORENSTEIN

PHOTO COURTESY OF ATARA

There is a quiet but powerful realization that is becoming apparent to more and more women.

A life of *Torah* is not meant to mute what *H-shem* has placed within us. It is meant to guide it, shape it, and elevate it. The talents we carry are not separate from our spiritual lives. They are part of them. The path is not always immediately clear.

It asks us to grow, to question, and to discover how our gifts can live within *Torah*, not only personally but professionally. Within that search lies a grounding truth: nothing we have been given is accidental. *H-shem* gives each ability with intention. When aligned with *Torah*, those gifts become more focused, more meaningful, and ultimately more impactful.

TZIONA ACHISHENA I 2018 ISRAEL I COURTESY OF ATARA

Over the years, I have had the privilege of working alongside the founders of ATARA: The Arts and *Torah* Association, through different collaborations. Through newsletters, conferences, curated platforms, and creative initiatives, ATARA has created a space where women can develop their artistic voice with clarity, integrity, and professional excellence, while remaining deeply connected to *Torah* values. For there was never an issue of choosing one over the other.

H-shem wants us to bring them together, fully and beautifully.

ATARA
THE ARTS AND TORAH
ASSOCIATION
elevating the arts

THE STORY BEHIND ATARA

In 2006, in Boston, Miriam Leah Gamliel and Esther Leah Marchette connected over music at a *Shabbat* table and recognized a void. There was no clear path for women to pursue artistic excellence within a *Torah* framework. That same year, as a first step, they began with a women-only performance at Stern College.

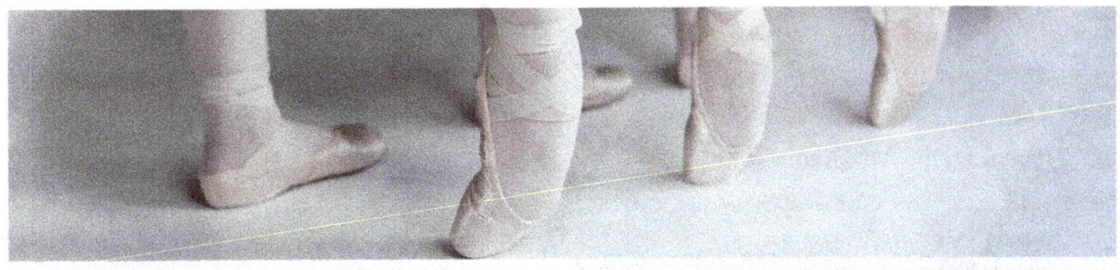

They reached out across cities and countries, and with a small team of volunteers, gathered women who had felt isolated as artists to create a community. Women shared talent in music and dance performance, acting improv and more. What emerged was not just an event, but the revelation of a real and widespread need.

ATARA grew organically from there. Conferences followed, creating not only opportunities to perform and learn, but spaces for connection. Women found peers, partners, and a shared sense of direction. Over time, it evolved into a network rather than a central institution. Today, ATARA connects *Torah*-observant women artists across and within disciplines, united by their commitment to *Torah* and to developing their craft with depth, integrity, and professionalism.

MEET THE FOUNDERS

What is the biggest challenge faced by Jewish women in the arts today?

E.L: Jewish women often carry full lives of work, family, and community, which can limit the time and space available for creative growth. Beyond this practical reality, there is also the inner work of trusting one's own soul. I would love to see even more religious Jewish artists feel free to create work that is emotionally honest and spiritually alive, taking risks in personal expression and creative experimentation while remaining rooted in *Torah*.

What is the most powerful aspect of being an artist within a Torah framework?

M.L.: Melody, story, and imagery move emotions in ways that words alone cannot. The arts are so impactful that artists are often described as change agents. If that is true, if we are gifted with the ability to communicate in powerful emotional languages, then, as *Torah* artists our work has the potential to influence the world toward something higher, more spiritual, and more aligned with *Torah* values.

E.L: The power lies in both differentiation and harmony. Each of us is a uniquely shaped instrument. *Torah* does not erase individuality. It refines it. When creativity becomes an act of *avoda*, our distinct voices can come together to form something greater than any one of us alone.

What does ATARA mean to you personally?

E.L.: For me, ATARA has been a labor of love. I care deeply about fostering connection and support for women across the full spectrum of creative expression, whether in the richness of performance or in the more healing and transformational side of art that resonates personally with me.

M.L.: I see it almost as a *shadchan* for artists. It brings people together. When artists unite, something larger can happen. Our success is seeing that we have become greater than the sum of our parts.

How do you balance your personal artistic pursuits with supporting ATARA?

M.L.: Balance hasn't come easily. For years, much of our energy went into building community rather than pursuing our own personal work. Recently, I've returned to my own creative life in Montreal, directing a Sunday performing arts program, hosting open mic nights and concerts, and helping launch a local theater initiative. I am now beginning to write and record my own music.

E.L.: For many years, while working full time in a demanding job and caring for my family, my creative life unfolded in quieter ways, through *hitbodedut*, personal prayer, teaching, music, and deep conversations shared in intimate settings. Supporting other artists has also been a form of creative expression for me. I am now working on a *Breslov niggun* recording project rooted in decades of lived practice, while also making space for new forms of expression.

When you stepped away from secular performance environments, what part of your identity felt most shaken?

M.L.: I literally gave up my entire identity. I had studied performing arts and didn't know who I was supposed to be anymore. At the time, it felt like part of *teshuva*. I stopped singing without fully understanding priority distinctions between *kashrus* and *kol isha*. No one explained otherwise, and I accepted that *H-shem* knew better than I did. Only years later, hearing the pain in other women's journeys, I began to understand it differently. That experience gave me the ability to truly relate to others going through similar struggles.

What kind of internal conflict do women artists carry, and how can that shift toward refinement?

M.L.: There are questions like, how do I use my talent, and why do I have it? There is a layer of existential struggle. Many feel that their skills do not have a clear place. The first step is recognizing that this is not unique to religious artists. Any artist can have these questions. But for us as *ovdei H-shem*, we can actually feel blessed — *H-shem* chose us to serve Him in a unique way and gave us what we need to accomplish our specific mission - we can practice "*aseh tov*" with our art.

E.L.: *H-shem* gives talents for a reason. When aligned with *Torah*, art becomes one of the most powerful ways to teach, heal, inspire, and bring joy. It can reach people in ways that other mediums cannot.

LOOKING AHEAD

ATARA is developing an Artist Finder directory to help communities connect with teachers and performers, creating greater access and sustainable opportunities. They currently offer small interest groups based on art domain and location, and keep the community updated with inspiring new work in the arts. They may renew in-person gatherings, intimate spaces where women can learn, connect, and experience live performance with the same energy and authenticity their conferences have always carried.

Miriam Leah Gamliel is the founder and director of ATARA: The Arts & *Torah* Association. Trained in musical theater, she creates and directs productions in Montreal and leads women's artistic collaborations. A former librarian and academic scholar, she holds an EdD from YU and **is a mother.**

Annie Orenstein is a producer dedicated to creating performance spaces for Jewish women and girls since 2006. Co-founder of *Spotlight On Women*, she has produced dozens of open mics, hosted Spotlight On Women radio, and currently writes about artists. She lives in Maaleh Adumim with her family.

Esther Leah (Aviva) Marchette is co-founder of ATARA. A singer, songwriter, former cantor and Berklee College of Music graduate, she focuses on prayer-centered musical expression. She works in music technology, teaches *Breslov* classes in Boston, and is recording a *niggun* album.

Stay Connected

Subscribe to *The High Notes* newsletter

🌐 **artsandtorah.org**

The Jewish Women's Playlists
youtube.com/@
▶ **JewishWomensPlaylists**

Alongside its founders, ATARA is supported by a leadership and advisory network including Henya Storch, Toby Klein Greenwald, Bracha Goetz, Chaya Bracha Rubin, Keri Roth, Nechama Leah Dahan, Robyn Shrater Seemann, Yona Lavie, Abigail H. Meyer, Ayala Feingold, Jessica Mzhen, Gayle Asch, Mark Finkel, Ron Ashkenas and others who help bring its vision to life. Much of ATARA's work has been volunteer-driven.

The coming year will mark 20 years of collaboration and ATARA's innovative initiatives unlocking the potential of *Torah*-aligned women's creativity.

EMUNAH ON CANVAS:
Simcha Even Chaim's Resilience

EXCLUSIVELY FOR HER TRIBE MAGAZINE

Simcha Even-Chaim's work lives where aesthetics meet *emunah*. Shaped by depth and resilience, her paintings move toward light with clarity and presence. There is a poetic, almost prayerful quality to her art—magnetic, guided by a clear *kavanah* in every detail.

Living just kilometers from Gaza, and having experienced the terror of October 7th firsthand, Simcha does not speak about faith from theory. She lives it. She paints it. She chooses it.

Can you take us back to the beginning—what shaped your connection to art?

My story begins in a difficult place. When I was growing up, my brother was a very talented artist, known not only in Israel but around the world. I grew up surrounded by his work and presence. When I was 17, my brother left this world. It was a deep trauma for me and for my family.

We did not grow up with *emunah*. My mother was traditional, lighting *Shabbat* candles, but we did not have answers to deeper questions. My brother had a very gentle soul and carried many questions—why life is so difficult, why there is so much pain, why good people suffer. Life was very hard for him. When he was no longer here, everything changed. One day you have a brother, and the next day he is gone. I began asking myself: What is life?

What happens after someone leaves the world?

At first, I thought I was speaking only to him. Slowly, I understood I was speaking to *H-shem*. I was asking: Why? Where is he now? Through this, I discovered that I have a soul, not just a body. And my brother's soul did not end when his body was gone.

When did painting itself become part of your life in a real way?

I missed my brother deeply. I would spend long moments looking at his paintings, and after some time, I felt a strong urge to paint as well. It was an impulsive pull that drew me into it.

I took his oil paints—still soft and usable—and simply began to paint using his colors and brushes. I was amazed that my first painting looked like the work of someone who had been painting for many years. I immediately understood that it was a gift I had received from his soul, flowing through me. I began painting with them. At first, I painted pain. I used very dark colors and placed everything onto the canvas—the grief, the longing, everything inside me.

At one point, I stopped painting completely for six months. I did not touch a brush. I felt that if *H-shem* gave me such a gift, I could not use it only for darkness.

During that time, I began learning *Torah*. Then something opened, like a window in my mind. I understood that art has a deeper purpose—it can lift, connect, and carry one beyond the moment.

My name is Simcha. I felt I could not create only sadness. I wanted to create light—something that gives strength. So I made a decision: my art will not stay in darkness.

When I returned to painting, everything changed. When I paint, I feel like a channel. I do not always know what I will paint. I begin, and then it comes. Painting is a way to connect, without words, to the Creator through the heart. My intention is that anyone who looks at my work can experience that connection for themselves.

October 7th changed so many lives. Can you take us back to that day?

I live seven kilometers from Gaza. Very close.

That morning, everything changed in one moment. We heard loud explosions. The house was shaking. Pictures were falling. It felt like going from normal life into darkness in a second.

A huge explosion followed right outside our home. We ran out. There was fire everywhere. No phone, no information. I did not know where my husband or my children were. You just run. Later, when we came back, the street was blackened, the houses damaged—and still, I was alive. My children were alive. My husband was alive. Slowly, I saw all of them coming back, and we cried, saying, "Thank You, thank You—we are alive."

You are in shock, but within that shock, you understand that you have experienced a very big miracle. We witnessed so many miracles, and it required deep faith to move through that time without breaking.

After that, we went to stay with family, then to Jerusalem. Because of the war and the damage in our area, we could not return home and were away for about two months. During that time, we experienced a lot of *chesed.* People supported us in simple ways, and it meant everything. You feel that you are not alone.

One of the paintings I created shows the Land of Israel with pain, and next to it a soldier wrapped in *tefillin.* For me, it represents the strength of our people—to continue believing even through suffering.

Many people might ask, how can you still feel this is the right place for you to live?

People who live here feel something that others may not feel in the same way. You see it with your own eyes, and you feel inside how *H-shem* is with you.

This is my country. This is my ground. We built our home here, in this holy land. Why should I leave it? Because of fear? No. I believe *H-shem* gave me this place. That is real *emunah.*

And what also gives strength is knowing that people around the world are thinking of us and standing with us.

You mentioned a dream that deeply impacted your path. Can you share it?

Yes. I had a dream of *geulah.* A real dream. I saw many circles of people dancing—circles within circles, like a mandala. The whole world was filled with light. It was all of *Am Yisrael,* dancing and singing. I did not only see it—I heard it.

Even after I woke up, I could still hear the singing. It was very strong. Later, I understood that it was *geulah*. After that, my painting changed. I began painting light—the *Beit HaMikdash*, and scenes from *Torah*.

You sometimes include yourself in your paintings. Why?

Painting helped me reconnect with myself. It gave me a way to express everything without words. In Hebrew, *panim* means face, but also inside—*penimiyut*.

When I paint a face, I am not only painting how it looks. I am painting what is inside. The eyes are like windows to the soul. Through painting, I began to discover my own soul. It became part of my healing.

You live close to Baba Sali. What does that connection mean to you?

I live close to Baba Sali, and I feel it is a great *hashgacha*. I feel very close to him and connected to his soul. I usually begin my day with morning *tefillah* at his *kever*, and it gives me strength for the entire day. I believe his presence brings protection, and especially on October 7th, there was a strong feeling of protection from above. *Baruch H-shem*.

Can you say more about *emunah*, for someone who is struggling?

I also ask.

But inside, I believe this is part of a bigger story that *H-shem* is writing. From *Bereishit* until now, we are inside it.

I am not here to change everything. I do what I can, and I let *H-shem* lead. I understand the questions. I really do. But inside, I choose to believe. We are not here to understand everything. We are here to bring light where we can. And sometimes, that light begins with one small choice—to keep going, to believe, to hold on.

What does *Shavuot* mean to you?

I feel a deep connection to *Shavuot*. I was born in the month of *Sivan*, which makes it especially meaningful to me. The story of *Ruth* inspires me deeply. She sees where the light is and follows it with strength. That is something I connect to in my life and express in my art—following the light, even when the path is not easy.

Simcha Even-Chaim is an Israeli artist whose work is shaped by a journey of loss, searching, and return to *Torah*. Inspired by the teachings of *Rebbe Nachman of Breslov*, her paintings channel *emunah*, healing, and a deep connection to *H-shem*.

🌐 simcha-art.co.il

📷 @simcha.evenhaim

Malka Safier: Where Color and *Torah* Meet the Soul

EXCLUSIVELY FOR HER TRIBE MAGAZINE

There is a richness to Malka Safier's work that you feel before you even understand it. Her paintings carry a quiet confidence — layered, intentional, and deeply rooted in something real. With bold color and textured depth, she brings moments of *Torah*, memory, and emotion onto the canvas in a way that feels both personal and expansive. It is not about following a style, but about honoring a voice. As we step into this conversation, we meet not only an artist, but a woman creating with clarity, purpose, and heart.

Can you take us back to the beginning? How did your journey into art start? Was there a defining moment?

My journey into art started when I was six years old. My mother saw early on that I loved colors and creating, so she sent me to formal art classes. I began with acrylics and painted for several years, and by the age of twelve I was already the youngest student in an oil painting class, surrounded by women in their fifties. I didn't think of it as something unusual at the time—it was simply something I loved and naturally gravitated toward.

What techniques are you most drawn to today, and what does your creative process look like?

Today I am most drawn to oil painting, especially working with rich, vibrant colors and thick textures. I want the viewer not only to see the artwork, but to feel it and experience it. Oil paints allow for a depth and longevity that is unmatched—many masterpieces last for centuries without fading, and that sense of timelessness is something I'm drawn to.

I also intentionally build texture into my work. It brings a modern dimension to traditional subjects and creates a more immersive experience.

My inspiration often begins long before I touch the canvas. It can come from hearing a new medrash, an insight into a biblical scene, or even from Jewish music. When I hear a song or a *tefila* that resonates deeply, something awakens in me, and that emotional and spiritual connection becomes the starting point of a painting.

Can you share your transition from painting for personal enjoyment to doing it professionally?

For many years, painting was something I did for myself, for my family, and for my home. I took art classes for about fifteen years, but I didn't see it as a career path.

After getting married, my husband and I lived in Yerushalayim while he learned in the Mir Yeshiva. During that time, I pursued a degree in social work and worked as a therapist in Israel. I worked in a high school and later at the family institute in Neve Yerushalayim. That was my professional identity for years.

The shift toward art happened gradually, but there was a moment that made me pause. A family member who is an art collector asked me to create a commissioned piece in a specific style. When I saw my work displayed in his home alongside other notable artworks, something changed. I remember thinking, "My artwork is valued. Maybe I'm onto something."

That thought stayed with me.

What makes your work unique in a world full of Judaic art?

From the beginning, I made a conscious decision not to mimic what already exists. I didn't want to create generic Judaic pieces. In fact, I avoided looking at other Judaic art online so I wouldn't be influenced by it.

Instead, I focused on developing my own voice. I often incorporate mefarshim and sometimes pesukim into my work,

adding layers of meaning that reflect my personal understanding and connection to the scene.

Another area where I feel my work is unique is in my family portraits. I create large-scale extended family paintings that include grandparents, married children, and grandchildren. One of the pieces I created included fifty-six people. I've never seen that done in this way before. It's incredibly meaningful to create something so personal that becomes a lasting treasure for a family.

What advice would you give women who want to bring meaningful art into their homes?

I always say to invest in artwork that holds meaning for you—something that you will continue to appreciate over time, beyond just aesthetics. Trends come and go, and sometimes pieces are chosen simply because they match the furniture. There's nothing wrong with that, as long as you feel a connection to it.

Your home is a reflection of who you are. The artwork you choose gives your space personality. It's almost like your walls are speaking, telling the story of what matters to your family.

MALKA SAFIER I SHIVAS HAMINIM I MALKASAFIERART.COM

Can you share the story behind your *Har Sinai* back cover piece?

For me, what differentiates an artist is not just the ability to paint with their hands, but to paint with their heart.

I clearly remember what inspired this piece. I was in my studio one day with music playing, and the song "From the Ashes" by Abie Rotenberg came on. I had never fully listened to the lyrics before, but that time, I was overwhelmed with emotion.

The song speaks about loss and about a generation that lifted themselves up from the dust. Three of my grandparents were Holocaust survivors, and I was very close to them. As I listened, I felt a deep personal connection and began to cry.

Then the final stanza described standing at a mountain, where our nation was founded, with faith etched into our hearts. That moment struck me deeply. Ma'amad *Har Sinai* is what defines us as a nation. It is the moment that gave us our connection to *H-shem* and instilled within us *bitachon*—the ability to endure and rise above hardship.

That became the inspiration for my *Har Sinai* painting. The vibrant colors reflect the joy, awe, and spiritual elevation of that moment. It represents the eternal bond between *Am Yisrael* and the Creator, and the strength that continues to carry us through every generation.

What do you love most about *Shavuot*?

I think there is something very deep about *Shavuot* that connects to every Jew, even if we don't always articulate it.

We all carry a longing for *Olam Haba* and *Gan Eden*, but how can we truly long for something we've never experienced?

I once heard from Rabbi Efraim Wachsman that this longing comes from *Matan Torah*. At *Har Sinai*, we experienced a level of clarity and closeness to *H-shem* that transcended the physical world. Even though it was a brief moment, it left a lasting imprint on every *neshama*.

Our souls remember that closeness. That's why the longing exists. It's really a desire to return to that state, to that connection, to that truth that we once experienced so clearly.

Can you share a moment of *hashgacha pratit* that shaped your path?

After several years working as a therapist, we moved to America, and I planned to take a break from seeing clients to help my children adjust to their new environment.

The home we moved into in Monsey had an art studio built into the garage. It felt like more than a coincidence, but I wasn't sure yet what it meant.

I started painting again, this time just experimenting and creating on my own. Within a short time, I began receiving calls from people who wanted to see my work, purchase pieces, and even take classes.

It became very clear to me that this was *hashgacha pratit*. Only *H-shem* could have orchestrated it in such a precise way.

It wasn't easy to step away from a career I had invested so much in, but I realized that this was a gift. Using a talent that felt so natural and innate was something I couldn't ignore.

It felt as if *H-shem* was telling me, "Don't worry, this is what you need to do now." That clarity is something I am deeply grateful for.

Tell us about your involvement in chesed and what drives it.

My connection to *chesed*, specifically with *Menucha V'Yeshua*, comes from a place of deep *hakaras hatov* to *H-shem*. I feel incredibly grateful that I have a career that I love and that allows me to bring joy to others.

After returning to *Eretz Yisrael* for *Sukkot* following the events of October 7, I felt a strong need to give back to the families most affected, especially the *almanos* and *yesomim*.

I wanted to use my art in a meaningful way, so I created a painting of the *shivas haminim* and paired it with a *dvar Torah* connecting *Am Yisrael* and the *chayalim hakedoshim* to its symbolism. We prepared and framed 250 pieces and distributed them to families during *Chol Hamoed*.

It was an incredibly emotional experience. We came thinking we would bring comfort and support, but we left feeling strengthened by them—by their courage, their *mesiras nefesh*, and their resilience.

That experience stayed with me. It reminded me that art is not just about beauty—it's about connection, about giving, and about using what we have been given to uplift others

Malka Safier is a Monsey-based Judaic artist known for her richly layered oil paintings that bring *Torah* narratives to life. With over fifteen years of artistic training, her work blends vibrant color, texture, and depth, drawing on *Tanach* and the beauty of *Eretz Yisrael* to create meaningful, timeless pieces.
🌐 **Malkasafierart.com**

Light, Nourishing Recipes for a Balanced Yom Tov

BY: DALIA BRUNSCHWIG

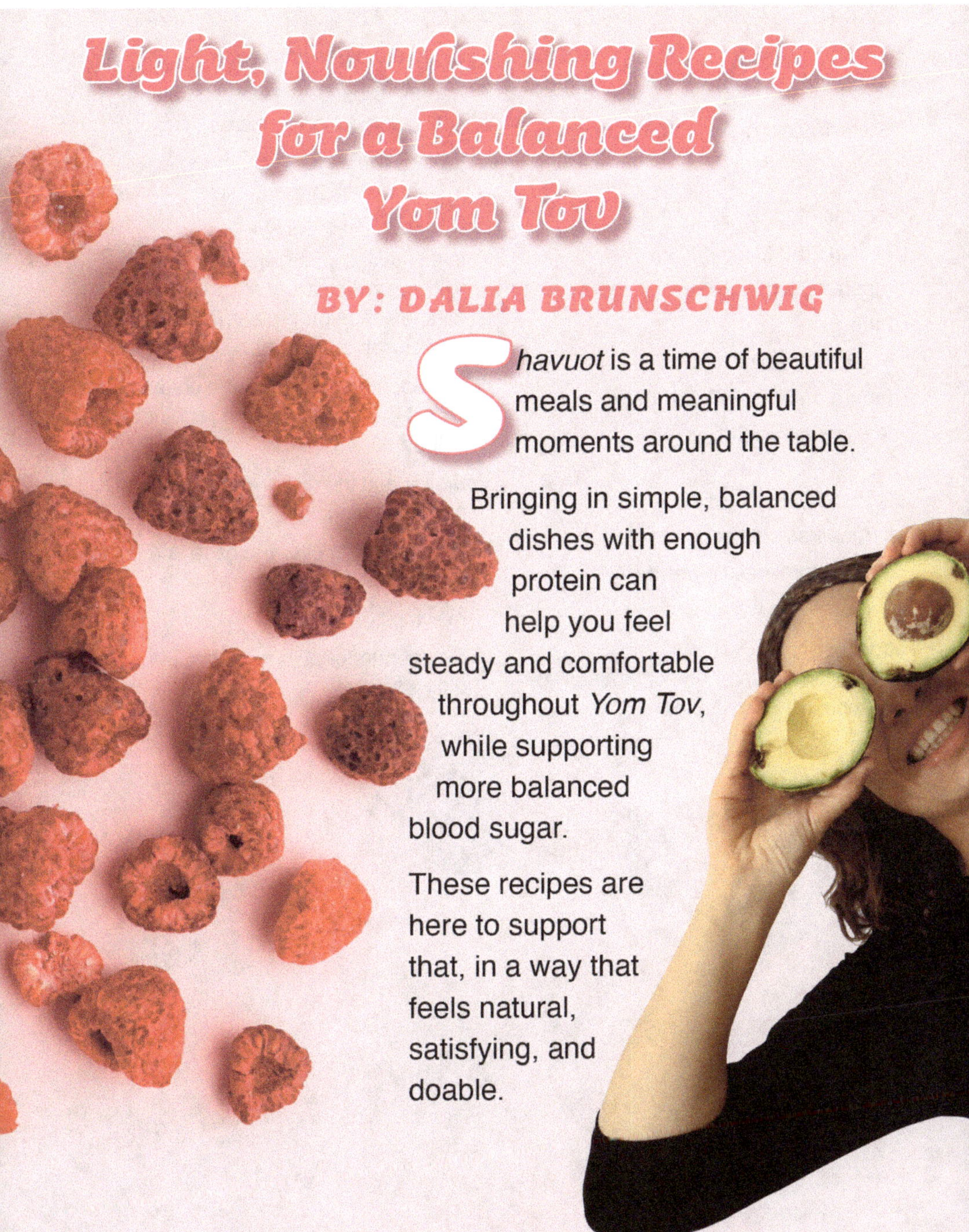

Shavuot is a time of beautiful meals and meaningful moments around the table.

Bringing in simple, balanced dishes with enough protein can help you feel steady and comfortable throughout *Yom Tov*, while supporting more balanced blood sugar.

These recipes are here to support that, in a way that feels natural, satisfying, and doable.

LIGHT CHEESECAKE (NO-BAKE)

Serves 4
Fits a 16 cm / 6-inch round form

Base:
6 dates (approx. 90 g / 3 oz)

¾ cup ground almonds
(approx. 75 g / 2.6 oz)

Filling:
¾ cup soft white cheese
(approx. 180 g / 6.3 oz)

½ cup plain yogurt
(approx. 120 g / 4.2 oz)

2 Tbsp honey

1 Tbsp fresh lemon juice

1 tsp natural gelatin powder

2 Tbsp warm water

Topping:
1 cup fresh raspberries or blueberries
(approx. 150 g / 5.3 oz)

Directions

Blend the dates until sticky.

Add the ground almonds and blend until a soft dough forms.

Press evenly into the base of a 16 cm / 6-inch round mold, or divide into small cups.

In a small bowl, mix the gelatin with warm water. Let sit for 1–2 minutes, then gently warm until fully dissolved. Do not boil.

In a separate bowl, mix the cheese, yogurt, honey, and lemon juice until smooth.

Slowly add the dissolved gelatin while mixing continuously.

Pour the filling over the base and smooth the top.

Add the berries.

Refrigerate for at least 3–4 hours, until fully set.

PHOTO BY DINAH ALTMAN

CHICKPEA CURRY

Serves 3

Ingredients

1 can coconut milk (400 ml / 13.5 oz)

2 Tbsp curry powder

½ tsp turmeric

3 cups broccoli, chopped
(approx. 300 g / 10.5 oz)

1 cup carrots, thinly sliced
(approx. 120 g / 4 oz)

1 cup cabbage, sliced
(approx. 90 g / 3 oz)

1½ cups cooked chickpeas
(approx. 250 g / 8.8 oz)

2 tsp lime juice

½ tsp sea salt, or to taste

Fresh basil, chopped (optional)

Directions

Heat a pan over medium heat.

Add the coconut milk, curry powder, and turmeric. Stir well and bring to a gentle boil.

Lower the heat and let simmer for 5 minutes.

Add the broccoli, carrots, cabbage, and chickpeas.

Cover and cook for 8–10 minutes, until the vegetables are tender.

Stir in the lime juice and salt.

Garnish with fresh basil, if desired.

Serve on its own, or with rice or cauliflower rice.

PHOTO BY DALIA BRUNSCHWIG

SALMON PATTIES

Serves 3

Ingredients

180 g raw salmon, skinless and boneless (6.3 oz)

½ cup onion, finely diced (approx. 75 g / 2.6 oz)

½ cup red bell pepper, finely diced (approx. 75 g / 2.6 oz)

½ cup celery, finely diced (approx. 60 g / 2.1 oz)

2 Tbsp fresh parsley, chopped

1 tsp garlic powder

1 Tbsp mustard

½ tsp ground black pepper

½ cup almond flour or oat flour (approx. 50 g / 1.8 oz)

2 eggs, lightly beaten

Olive oil or spray

Directions

Preheat the oven to 200°C (400°F). Line or grease a baking sheet.

In a bowl, flake the salmon.

Add the vegetables, parsley, and all remaining ingredients. Mix well.

Divide into 9 equal portions and shape into patties.

Place on the baking sheet and lightly brush or spray with olive oil.

Bake for 20 minutes, turning once halfway through.

Serve warm with a fresh salad or cooked vegetables.

Dalia Brunschwig is a Certified Integrative Nutrition Health Coach helping Jewish women achieve sustainable weight loss and healthier lifestyles within the rhythm of real life and Jewish traditions. Her work focuses on balance, simplicity, and self-awareness, creating supportive, judgment-free communities that empower women to stay accountable and build lasting, realistic habits.

hello@fullyinbalance.com

fullyinbalance.com

Two Simple Shavuot Wellness-ish Recipes

BY: YSANNE SPEVACK

For gluten-free, allergy-friendly wheat options, look no further than wheatgrass, which doesn't contain any grains. The grain starts to form 10 weeks after germination, so before that, there's zero gluten. Wheatgrass juice is a highly nutritious, enzyme-rich addition to your *Shavuot* diet plan, as well as being hydrating and stabilizing blood sugar, which is clearly needed to balance the cheesecake!

The chlorophyll supports digestion, vitamin C and other antioxidants boost the immune system, and flavonoids help fight inflammation. It also costs less than a shekel per glass. But if you don't see this in time to grow your own, don't worry—wheatgrass juice is also a great way to get your digestion back in shape after *Shavuot*.

Shavuot Sameach and *L'Chaim!*

Wheatgrass Juice

Ingredients:

½ cup whole wheat grains (wheat groats), preferably organic

Water

Potting soil

Method:

Soak the grains overnight in a cup of water, set in a warm cupboard away from direct light, for at least 12 hours and up to 24 hours.

Rinse with fresh cold water, return the clean, wet grains to the cup, and place back in the warm, dark cupboard. Repeat the process the next day.

After 1–2 days, tiny white roots will emerge from most of the grains. Carefully remove any grains that don't show emerging roots.

Spread potting soil on a small tray, about 2–3 cm deep.

Scatter the sprouted grains evenly across the surface, spacing them roughly ½ cm apart.

Cover with a very thin layer of soil, just enough to fully cover them.

Gently press down slightly so the soil makes contact with the grains above and below.

Carefully water the surface using a watering can with a rose, creating a gentle sprinkle rather than a strong stream.

Place the tray back in a warm cupboard for a few days. Keep the soil slightly moist, avoiding overwatering.

In 2–3 days, the grass will be about 2–5 cm tall. At that point, move the tray to a counter away from direct sunlight.

Continue to keep the soil moist (not wet), and the grass will be ready to harvest in 10–14 days.

Now for the juice:
Using a pestle and mortar, crush freshly cut wheatgrass with a small amount of cold water to extract the juice.

Pour off the first pressing into a glass. Add a little more water, crush again, and repeat this process three times.

A handful of wheatgrass is enough for one serving, as this juice is taken as a shot, not a full cup.

Make only what you need fresh, as it quickly loses its nutritional value.

No-Bake Vegan Strawberry Cheesecake

This quick and easy dessert is made with silken tofu and topped with fresh strawberries. It's an indulgent, decadent treat that connects with the *Ashkenazi* custom of serving dairy foods on *Shavuot*, including cheesecake.

Enjoy the tradition while skipping the dairy for a cleaner, lighter approach. That said, Lotus Biscoff biscuits aren't exactly "clean," but this is a realistic, crowd-pleasing recipe for any *Shavuot* table. They are kosher and vegan, even if high in sugar. The topping helps balance some of that sweetness.

I do believe in sometimes making foods that carry cultural comfort and are easy for everyone in the family to enjoy—and this is one of them. If you prefer, you can replace Lotus biscuits with any other kosher vegan option, including homemade ones.

Guten apetit / b'teavon!

RECIPE COURTESY OF YSANNE SPEVACK

No-Bake Vegan Strawberry Cheesecake

Ingredients

For the base:
250g Lotus Biscoff cookies

100g vegan butter

For the topping:
500g fresh strawberries, washed, halved, and dehulled

2 tbsp brown sugar

100g vegan white chocolate

350g silken tofu, drained

$\frac{2}{3}$ cup honey, maple syrup, or agave syrup

2 cups cashews, soaked in boiling water for one hour

Juice and zest of one lemon

1 tbsp vanilla extract

Base:
Line a 20 cm springform tin with baking paper on the bottom and sides.

Melt the vegan butter in a heatproof bowl over simmering water.

Place the biscuits in a ziplock bag (unsealed) and crush them using a rolling pin or bottle until fine crumbs form.

Transfer crumbs to a bowl, add melted butter, and mix well.

Press firmly into the base of the pan and refrigerate to set.

Topping:
Mix strawberries with sugar and set aside to macerate.

Melt the chocolate and set aside.

Add the remaining ingredients to a bowl and blend (in batches if needed) until smooth.

Stir in the melted chocolate.

Pour the mixture over the base, smooth the top, and refrigerate for at least one hour.

To serve, remove from the tin, place on a serving platter, and top with strawberries.

Let sit at room temperature for about an hour before serving.

(More info about Ysanne can be found on page 33.)

From Idea to Impact

How I Turn VISION Into REAL, INVESTABLE STARTUPS

BY: DR. AVITAL BECK

YOU ARE THE STARTUP

Before I even speak about startups, I always say the same thing: **you are the startup**.

People ask me how I manage everything, companies, business development, teaching, community, and a family with seven children. But it is not really about managing. It is about capacity. If your bucket is empty, nothing will grow. Many women are used to giving first and filling themselves last. But without energy, clarity, and inner strength, nothing sustainable can be built; not a business, not a family, not a long-term vision.

So the first stage is not strategy. It is self-development. You build your mindset, your body, your discipline. You learn how to create energy, not just spend it. For me, that meant systems. Waking up earlier over time. Moving my body every morning. Structuring my day with intention. It started small. Ten minutes earlier. One minute of movement, then two. Gradual, consistent growth. Without this foundation, nothing else holds.

A CLEAR VISION CREATES DIRECTION

Once the internal foundation is in place, direction becomes possible. I always ask one question: **what is your North Star?**

Not "What sounds good? What feels realistic? What do you actually want? You need a clear picture of where you are going. A business, a lifestyle, a level of impact. Without that, you are simply moving without direction.

I used to visualize very specific outcomes, even when reality looked completely different. I returned to that vision again and again. That is what builds will, a will changes everything. Once the vision is clear, you do not wait for it; you grow into it. If you want to be a CEO, act like one. If you want to build something significant, start behaving like someone who can carry that responsibility. Identity comes before outcome.

REALITY CHECK: DOES THIS IDEA MATTER

This is where many ideas fall apart. Passion matters. But it is not enough.

You need to ask real questions:
Is there a real problem?
Do people actually feel it?
Are they already trying to solve it?

The only way to know is to go out and ask. Speak to people outside your circle.

- ✓ Join relevant communities.
- ✓ Run simple surveys.
- ✓ Build a basic landing page and see if people respond. (In one of my first startups, we sent out a simple global form and gathered real data from women to understand the need.)
- ✓ Look at the competition. If there is none, it is usually not a good sign. It often means there is no real market. And one more critical point. Do not fall in love with technology. Something can be brilliant and still be unnecessary. People do not pay for innovation. They pay for solutions. If your product does not save time, reduce cost, or solve a real pain point, it will not work.

EXECUTION IS THE REAL DIFFERENTIATOR

Most ideas stop here. People wait for funding, for the perfect setup, and for certainty. Execution does not wait. In my first company, we needed a lab, equipment, and infrastructure. We had none of it. So we started anyway. We ordered basic materials online, ran small experiments, tested with people around us, and built a very simple prototype. It was far from perfect. But it was real. That is what matters. Start where you are. A simple version. One feature. A rough prototype. A first piece of content.

Investors do not invest in ideas. They invest in people who move.

BUILD MOMENTUM BEFORE YOU ASK FOR MONEY

Before you approach investors, you need evidence. Not perfection. Movement. A prototype. Conversations with experts. Feedback from users. Early partnerships. Even informal testing. If you can say, "I spoke to three doctors," or "someone already wants to join," you are no longer presenting an idea. You are showing traction. Investors are not the starting point. They amplify what is already in motion.

STAY FLEXIBLE AND FOLLOW WHAT WORKS

As you build, you will need to adjust. If something is not working, it does not mean failure. It means a change in direction. Many successful companies did not begin as what they eventually became. They discovered it along the way. Pay attention to what works. Sometimes the real opportunity is not where you started. If one part gains traction, focus there. Release what does not. Execution is not about forcing. It is about responding intelligently.

INVESTORS INVEST IN PEOPLE

When you enter investor meetings, there is a shift most founders do not expect. The meeting is not really about the business. It is about the relationship. Investors see many strong ideas. What they are deciding is whether they want to work with you. Connection matters. You cannot walk into a room only trying to sell. You need to listen, engage, and create a real interaction.

I have seen meetings where most of the time was spent talking about personal topics, and that was enough. The decision was already forming through the connection. The business still needs to make sense. But that is the baseline. The decision is often emotional.

REJECTION IS PART OF THE STRATEGY

You will hear "no" many times. Each "no" is information. Ask why. Learn from it. Take the insight and improve. And sometimes you will not even get a "no", you will get silence. That is harder. Follow up but bring something new. Progress, development, a new insight. Show movement. And do not take it personally. One person saying no does not define the idea. It simply means it is not right for them. Think in abundance! The next person will be the right fit and will love your idea!

BUILD THE RIGHT NETWORK

The first "yes" is the hardest, but once the first yes happens, everything shifts. Momentum builds. Confidence rises. Other investors begin to follow. That first yes is more than funding. It is validation. The right investors bring more than money. They bring experience, connections, and strategic value.

But before all of that, you need a network. And networks do not start big. They start with one person. In my case, I knew one person connected to the startup world. I asked for help. That led to another introduction, and then another.

That is how it grows. You ask, you connect, you continue. At the core, everything works in cycles. You give, you grow, you give again. Sometimes the return is not immediate. But over time, it comes back. That is also why I wrote my book.

There came a point where I felt full. I had learned, experienced, and built so much, and I understood it cannot stay with me. It has to move forward. Because building a startup is not only about building something external. It is about becoming someone who creates, connects, gives, and continues to grow. And when you reach that place, the path does not end. That is where real impact begins.

Dr. Avital Beck is a scientist, serial entrepreneur, and CEO specializing in personal development and positive psychology grounded in brain science. A global speaker and workshop leader, she bridges science, spirituality, and practical tools to help individuals and organizations unlock potential, achieve peak performance, and build meaningful, successful lives

🌐 **YouAreTheStartUp.com**

🔺 **Startup Yourself**

Know Your Value:
A Woman's Guide to Earning Without Apology

BY: CHANY ROSENGARTEN

The Block Is Not the End

If things feel stuck for you financially, it is very easy to assume that something is wrong with you. That you are not capable enough, not consistent enough, or simply not someone for whom things work.

But that is usually not what is happening.

Most women are not starting from a neutral place when it comes to money. They are operating from patterns that were shaped long before they ever thought about pricing, business, or earning. These patterns come from what they saw growing up, what felt acceptable, what was encouraged, and what was quietly limited.

Over time, those messages become internal. They shape what feels realistic, what feels "too much," and what feels like it is simply not for you.

So when a woman says, "I tried everything," or "Nothing works for me," she is often not describing reality. She is describing a belief that has been reinforced over time.

That belief is the block, and as long as you believe it, you will keep recreating it.

You Are Not Limited, You Were Taught to Think That Way

At the same time, there is something deeper that needs to be understood.

You are not a limited being. You are a *neshama*, rooted in something infinite. Human potential is not small. If you can perceive something, it already exists as a possibility.

The tension many women feel comes from living between these two realities. On one hand, they carry unlimited potential. On the other, they have been trained to think in limited ways.

So even when opportunity is present, something inside says, "Not me."

That is not truth. That is learned limitation.

Why Money Feels So Complicated

Many women feel uncomfortable wanting more. Not only practically, but emotionally and even spiritually. It can feel "not *frum*," not refined, or not aligned with the kind of life they want to live.

But that discomfort does not come from *Torah*. It comes from what was absorbed along the way.

A *Yid* needs money. Life costs money. Raising children, running a home, giving, and living responsibly all require resources. Money is not separate from a meaningful life. It is part of it.

The discomfort is learned.

The Thoughts That Quietly Keep You Small

If you listen carefully, you will notice certain thoughts that repeat themselves.

"I can't have it all."
"If I have money, something else will suffer."
"If things feel good, something will go wrong."
"It's not right for me to want more."

These are not neutral thoughts. They are conclusions, often built on fear.

Sometimes there is also a deeper fear. If your life expands, will you still belong? Will you still feel connected to the people around you?

So instead of allowing growth, you limit yourself in advance.

Emunah offers a different perspective. *H-shem* is good, and *H-shem* wants to give good. Your role is not to stay small to stay safe. Your role is to remain open.

Self-Respect Changes the Way You Decide

Many decisions around work and money are made from pressure.

A little money feels better than no money, so you take what is available. You say yes when something does not feel aligned. You lower your price to secure the opportunity.

These are survival decisions. And survival decisions keep you in survival.

When a woman begins to operate from self-respect, her decisions change before her circumstances do. She stops negotiating herself down in order to secure something, and starts responding from a place of inner stability.

What This Looks Like in Real Life

Read this slowly. Apply one at a time.

- ✓ You are not starting from nothing. You are someone H-ashem wants to give to.
- ✓ Capability is not the problem. Not seeing yourself is.
- ✓ A little money is not always the answer. Acting from pressure keeps you small.
- ✓ Your price is not a guess. You already feel when it is too low.
- ✓ Discomfort does not mean you are wrong. It means you are growing.
- ✓ Your client is not your source. They are a channel. H-shem is the source.
- ✓ You do not need to prove your value. You need to recognize it.
- ✓ It is normal to have enough. Let that become natural.
- ✓ You do not wait to become confident. You begin now.
- ✓ Reality is not against you. You act and still expand.
- ✓ You are not here only to give. You are meant to receive.

That is where real change begins.

Capability Is Not What Determines Income

Many women believe that income reflects capability.

It does not. Very often, women who feel less worthy become extremely capable. They overdeliver, overwork, and continue proving themselves.

And still, they undercharge.

Because the issue is not what you do. The issue is whether you see yourself clearly.

Do you even see yourself?

Because if you do not, your reality will reflect that, no matter how good you are.

A Practical Way to Think About Pricing

Pricing becomes clear when you stop treating it as a guessing game. Most women are not confused about pricing, they are disconnected from their own internal clarity.

If you move a number up and down, you can feel it. You can feel when it is too low. You can feel when it is too high. Somewhere in between, there is a number that feels both uncomfortable and true.

That discomfort is not a problem.

It is growth. Your body already knows.

Your Client Is Not Your Source

One of the most important shifts a woman can make is understanding where her money comes from.

117

The person in front of you is not your source. They are a channel. *H-shem* is the source.

When you believe your client is your source, you shrink. You overwork, undercharge, and compromise your boundaries.

When you understand that they are a channel, you stop performing and start relating. You can show up clearly, communicate honestly, and make decisions with dignity.

Reality Is Not a Punishment

Growth does not remove reality.

Bills still need to be paid. Responsibilities remain. You still take action.

But reality is not against you, and it is not a punishment. You do not put your life on hold while you are building it. You take responsibility, and at the same time, you allow yourself to expand.

Receiving Is Part of the Flow

Many women are very comfortable giving.

Receiving feels different. But life is not meant to move in one direction. You are meant to be sustained. If having enough feels unfamiliar, it is not because it is wrong. It is because it has not yet been normalized.

Part of the work is to allow it to feel natural to have enough.

The Work

This is not surface work.

It is the work of returning to who you are.

To self-respect. To self-love. To clarity.

Over time, something settles. Not because everything around you is perfect, but because you are no longer negotiating your worth. You begin to live from it.

And from that place, you start to experience something different. What you give is not lost. It returns. Not always in the same way, not always immediately, but consistently.

Because life is not meant to be only giving. There is a flow.

And you are meant to be sustained.

Chany Rosengarten is a mentor and educator focused on self-respect, emotional clarity, and building a grounded relationship with money and self-worth. Through her programs and teachings, she helps women move out of limitation into stability, confidence, and aligned *parnassah* rooted in *emunah*, dignity, and personal responsibility.

🌐 **gitty-chany-s-school.thinkific.com**
▶ **support@chanyrosengarten.com**